The Passion of God

The Passion of God

*Divine Suffering
in Contemporary
Protestant Theology*

Warren McWilliams

MⲨP MERCER UNIVERSITY PRESS

ISBN 0-86554-158-2

The Passion of God
Copyright © 1985 by
Mercer University Press, Macon GA 31207
All rights reserved
Printed in the United States of America

All books published by Mercer University Press are produced
on acid-free paper that exceeds the minimum standards set by the
National Historical Publications and Records Commission.

Library of Congress Cataloging in Publication Data
McWilliams, Warren, 1946–
    The passion of God.
    Includes index.
    1. Suffering of God—History of doctrines—20th
century.   I. Title.
BT153.S8M38   1985   231'.4   85-2892
    ISBN 0-86554-158-2 (alk. paper)

Table of Contents

Dedicated to

George and Werdna McWilliams
and
Arnold and Ruth Long

Preface

Does God suffer? To many Christians this question will seem strange and even irrelevant. Many Christians have wrestled with the problem of human suffering. Does God cause human suffering? Does God allow human suffering? These seem to be much more fundamental questions. In recent years, however, several theologians have argued that God suffers along with human beings in their suffering. A loving, compassionate God must identify with human misery.

Although many books have been devoted to the question of God's responsibility for human suffering, relatively few have been concerned with the question of divine suffering. The traditional issue of divine responsibility for suffering (theodicy) may be a more vital, experiential concern for many Christians, but the question of divine "passion" or suffering has provoked considerable discussion in the twentieth century. In fact, a recognition of divine suffering may be an intrinsic part of a comprehensive Christian response to the theodicy issue.

As far as I know, no one has attempted a systematic comparison and critique of the major contemporary proponents of divine suffering. As I explain more fully in the first chapter, I have chosen the six theologians treated in this study because they are deeply concerned with the question of divine suffering; they have written since World War II; they affirm divine suffering from a variety of theological perspectives; and they represent diverse geographical, ethnic, and denominational backgrounds. Instead of a comprehensive study of all major advocates of divine suffering, I have chosen some representative figures. Interacting with these should stimulate further discussion of this significant issue.

Although this work is primarily a study of academic theologians, I hope the reader will realize the question of divine suffering is not solely a concern of professional theologians. Perhaps lay people who have considered God's relationship to human suffering will find some helpful insights in this study. As I indicate in the final chapter, the issue of divine suffering compels us to reconsider the most fundamental theological issue of our day—the nature of God. The concluding chapter also includes an attempt to sketch out the implications of divine suffering for the Christian life.

I want to thank the publishers of several journals for allowing me to use material in this volume that appeared in slightly different form in their publications: *Encounter* for "The Passion of God and Moltmann's Christology," "Daniel Day Williams' Vulnerable and Invulnerable God," and "A Kenotic God and the Problem of Evil"; *Scottish Journal of Theology* for "Divine Suffering in Contemporary Theology"; *The Journal of Religious Thought* for "Theodicy according to James Cone"; and *Perspectives in Religious Studies* for "The Pain of God in the Theology of Kazoh Kitamori." Some portions of this book have been presented at professional meetings, where numerous colleagues clarified my thinking.

Finally, I want to thank my colleagues in the School of Christian Service for their encouragement as I prepared this manuscript. I express my gratitude also to the Oklahoma Baptist University administration for providing financial support for this project. My fellow pilgrims at University Baptist Church have often demonstrated to me how a community of faith responds to tragedy using the resources of the Christian tradition. I have dedicated this book to my parents and my in-laws. Their influence on my life is clear to me, and I understand the Christian response to suffering better because of them. Above all, I want to express my appreciation to my wife, Patty, and my two daughters, Amy and Karen, for their continuing support of my work. I constantly see reflected in their lives the compassion and love that characterizes the God of the Bible.

Warren McWilliams

Chapter One

The Passion
of God

What is God's relation to human suffering? Did God cause our suffering? Is some suffering due to human activity instead of divine? What is God doing to alleviate our suffering? Questions such as these have been perennial ones for the Christian faith. Human suffering seems to be an inescapable feature of human existence, and thoughtful Christians have always tried to interpret this experience within the context of their faith. For most Christians the main issue has been the extent to which God causes or allows human suffering. The theodicy issue is usually formulated in terms of an apparent dilemma. Is God (*theos*) just (*dike*)? If God is both good and powerful, why is there suffering? A good God would want to alleviate human misery, and a powerful God would exercise his power to achieve that end. Yet misery abounds. Just a few minutes ago I finished reading the morning newspaper. As usual almost every page recorded some instance of human anguish: tornadoes and floods hit the state last night, bringing destruction and death, car wrecks maimed and killed others, murders and rapes continued as usual, and various diseases forced more people into hospitals and convalescent homes. Experiences such as these continually raise the theodicy issue to the consciousness of Christians. Whether the suffering is called moral evil (e.g., man's inhumanity to man) or natural evil (leukemia, tornadoes, etc.), the questions remain: Is God responsible? Why did God create a world in which accidents and inhumanity are possible?

Although the theodicy issue has always perplexed Christians, another aspect of the problem of suffering has captured the attention of theologians in the last few years. Given that suffering is a fact of human existence, the general question is, How does God respond to human misery? The specific focus of the concern for some theologians has been, Does God suffer? Can God feel real pain, anguish, sorrow, or disappointment about the human predicament? The answer of most traditional Christian theists has been negative. The mainstream, orthodox list of divine attributes has normally included impassibility, that is, God cannot suffer.

Impassibility is derived from the Latin root *passio* (suffering), which is equivalent to the Greek pathēma and pathos. *Passio* was normally used in the Vulgate to translate pathēma and pathos. Pathos, for example, may refer to "that which is endured or experienced, *suffering*" (e.g., the "passion" of Christ), or to passion in the sense of immoral or inappropriate feelings or desires (e.g., lustful passions).[1] Impassibility is defined as "not capable of being affected or acted upon."[2] In this study "passion" will be used for God's capacity to suffer or be acted upon by the created order. As one writer put it: "He is without passions (with a small p) but not without Passion (with a capital letter): there is in Him what has been called the Divine Pathos."[3] Of the writers to be discussed in detail in this study, only Moltmann uses the category of "passion" in a systematic way, but others refer to God's pain, empathy, sorrow, sensitivity, suffering, pathos, or passibility. In orthodox theology three aspects of divine passibility were often distinguished and denied: "(1) external passibility or the capacity to be acted upon from without, (2) internal passibility or the capacity for changing the emotions from within, and (3) sensational passibility or the liability to feelings of pleasure and pain caused by the action of another

---

[1]W. F. Arndt and F. W. Gingrich, *A Greek-English Lexicon of the New Testament and Other Early Christian Literature* (Chicago: University of Chicago Press, 1957) 607-608. Cf. Abraham J. Heschel, *The Prophets*, vol. 2 (New York: Harper & Row, 1975) 269-72.

[2]Van A. Harvey, *A Handbook of Theological Terms* (New York: Macmillan, 1964) 129.

[3]Kenneth J. Woollcombe, "The Pain of God," *Scottish Journal of Theology* 20 (June 1967): 129.

being."[4] Many propassibility theologians in recent years have not responded directly to this particular threefold scheme, but they would apparently have no reluctance in attributing all three types of possibility to God.

Since the early nineteenth century, numerous theologians, biblical scholars, and philosophers of religion have criticized the doctrine of divine impassibility. Currently it is not surprising to find a theologian arguing this way: "The concept of divine suffering is not only the core of our faith but the uniqueness of Christianity."[5] More and more Christians are affirming divine passibility and criticizing divine impassibility, but only a few have developed the systematic consequences of such views. In 1963 Paul Tillich noted that most theologians "avoid the problem altogether, either by ignoring it or by calling it an inscrutable divine mystery."[6] Now, several years later, Tillich's judgment is only partially correct. More theologians are confronting the issue, but many still fail to explore the issue as carefully as necessary. The situation is better described as "theological brinksmanship."[7] The primary purpose of this study is to examine some of the prominent proponents of divine suffering in the last few decades. These are the thinkers who have been willing to leap beyond the brink and analyze a highly significant theological and practical issue.

One's conclusions about the suffering of God can have serious implications for all aspects of Christian faith and life. None of the contemporary theologians treated here would consider the issue esoteric and abstract. Indeed, they all see the affirmation of divine suffering as a crucial component in resolving the problem of human suffering. They generally find deep consolation in the aware-

---

[4]F. L. Cross and E. A. Livingstone, eds., *The Oxford Dictionary of the Christian Church*, 2d ed. (London: Oxford University Press, 1974) 694.

[5]Jung Young Lee, *God Suffers for Us: A Systematic Inquiry into a Concept of Divine Passibility* (The Hague: Martinus Nijhoff, 1974) 1.

[6]Paul Tillich, *Systematic Theology*, vol. 3 (Chicago: University of Chicago Press, 1963) 404.

[7]Woollcombe, "The Pain of God," 133.

ness of God's suffering with mankind. Quite often they insist that concern with the traditional theodicy issue is too speculative and abstract to be beneficial for suffering humanity. Rather than speculating about the origin of evil, the Bible stresses God's response to suffering. A key facet of that divine response, they argue, is his passion. Most would agree that divine passion is "the most profound of all responses to human anguish."[8]

BIBLICAL AND HISTORICAL PERSPECTIVES

Before presenting the attitudes of contemporary theologians on this issue, I will give brief attention to some of the biblical and historical background for the passibility-impassibility debate. No attempt will be made to be comprehensive on this material. Most of the contemporary theologians who affirm divine suffering treat this background in some detail. Here my concern is merely to sketch the major contours of the discussion.

One reason for the frequent debate over the impassibility of God is the kind of language used in the Bible to describe God. Many passages affirm the radical difference between divine and human natures (e.g., Isaiah 40:18,25; Hosea 11:9). Other texts freely use anthropomorphic language to describe God; in other words, human form is attributed to God. God walks, talks, smells, hears, writes, and has a back side that Moses can see. Especially important for the impassibility discussion are the passages that use anthropopathic language in attributing human feelings, moods, or emotions to God. For example, God loves, hates, is jealous, and is patient. Perhaps the classic example of the ambiguous or paradoxical nature of biblical language would be the numerous passages about the repentance of God, indicating a change in attitude or intention on his part (Genesis 6:6-7; Exodus 32:11-14; Judges 2:18; 1 Samuel 15:11,23; 2 Samuel 24:16; 1 Chronicles 21:15; Psalms 106:45; Jeremiah 18:8,10, 26:3,13,19, 42:10; Amos 7:3,6; Joel 2:13; Jonah 3:10, 4:2). Other passages, however, indicate that God does not change

---

[8]S. Paul Schilling, *God and Human Anguish* (Nashville: Abingdon Press, 1977) 235.

his mind and does not waver in the same way human beings do (Numbers 23:19; 1 Samuel 15:29; Psalms 110:4; Jeremiah 4:28; Zechariah 8:14-15; Malachi 3:6; James 1:17). These latter passages have been used to support the doctrine of God's immutability or unchangeableness, a belief often held in tandem with that of impassibility. In general, classical Christian theism has argued that passages with anthropomorphisms or anthropopathisms should be interpreted symbolically and that God's essential nature is unmarked by any human-resembling suffering or passion.[9]

Many proponents of divine passibility argue that the biblical view of God as a living, dynamic agent in history necessitates a suffering response to human misery. The biblical evidence on this topic is, however, open to diverse interpretations. One supporter of divine suffering says, "I do not know of a single text that one could invoke clearly and unequivocally to show that Scripture explicitly asserts the suffering of God."[10] Others would claim that the more natural reading of the Bible suggests divine suffering. For the sake of illustration, the Exodus event and Hebrew prophecy will be examined from the Old Testament.

The Exodus experience is often taken by the Hebrews as a paradigm for God's character and activity. God knows the Hebrews' situation in bondage and responds by liberating them (Exod. 2:23-25, 3:7-10). The clear implication is that God empathizes with their

---

[9]For brief discussions of the history of interpretation of God's repentance, see Lester J. Kuyper, "The Repentance of God," *The Reformed Review* 18 (May 1965): 3-16, and Lester J. Kuyper, "The Suffering and Repentance of God," *Scottish Journal of Theology* 22 (September 1969): 257-77. For histories of the doctrine of impassibility, see Gerald Wondra, "The Pathos of God," *The Reformed Review* 18 (December 1964): 28-35, and J. K. Mozley, *The Impassibility of God: A Survey of Christian Thought* (London: Cambridge University Press, 1926).

[10]Daniel Day Williams, "The Vulnerable and the Invulnerable God," *Christianity and Crisis* 22 (5 March 1962): 27. For recent discussions of the compassion or suffering of God in the Old Testament, see Claus Westermann, *Elements of Old Testament Theology*, trans. Douglas W. Stott (Atlanta: John Knox, 1982) 138-49; Terence E. Fretheim, *The Suffering of God: An Old Testament Perspective* (Philadelphia: Fortress Press, 1984).

suffering and responds out of that identification.[11] In addition, God is a jealous, impassioned covenant partner. One interpreter has even suggested that "YHWH," the name God announces to Moses in the burning-bush episode, denoted God's passionate commitment to his people. Yahweh is the passionate one.[12] Overall, unless one reads the Exodus story with divine impassibility assumed, the narrative would seem to support God's identification with the agony of the Hebrews. Later in their history, whenever the Hebrews faced adversity, they expected Yahweh to respond to their suffering and bring about a new Exodus. Certainly oppressed groups such as blacks often take the God of the Exodus as their rallying point.[13]

The Hebrew Prophets are often cited as supporters of divine passion. Abraham Heschel has written cogently and at great length on the pathos of God in the Prophets. God reacts with pain and sorrow to the Hebrews' breaking of the covenant. God's pathos "is not a passion, an unreasoned emotion, but an act founded with intention, rooted in decision and determination. . . ."[14] God's pathos is grounded in his intimate, personal relationship to the covenant community. Heschel notes the prevalence of anthropomorphic descriptions of God in the Prophets, and argues that these are central to the entire biblical message. He argues that the Prophets are often misunderstood because of a fear of anthropopathisms and the unfortunate influence of Greek philosophy on the interpretation of Scripture. Heschel recognizes, however, the limits of anthropopathisms in light of God's transcendence. He paraphrases Isaiah 55:8-9: "For My pathos is not your pathos, neither are your ways

---

[11]See, for example, George A. F. Knight, *Theology as Narration: A Commentary on the Book of Exodus* (Grand Rapids: William B. Eerdmans, 1976) 14, 19.

[12]S. D. Goitein, "YHWH the Passionate: The Monotheistic Meaning and Origin of the Name YHWH," *Vetus Testamentum* 6 (January 1956): 1-9.

[13]James H. Cone, *A Black Theology of Liberation* (Philadelphia: J. B. Lippincott, 1970) 18-19.

[14]Heschel, *The Prophets*, 11.

My ways, says the Lord. For as the heavens are higher than the earth, so are My ways higher than your ways, and My pathos than your pathos."[15] Although divine pathos is ultimately a mystery, the category is used by the Prophets to point to the dynamic, personal character of God's interaction with the Hebrews. Harold Knight followed Heschel's lead in stressing the suffering of God in the Prophets, describing God as "the greatest sufferer of all, because He alone can realize the true spiritual repercussions of the drama of human history."[16]

J. K. Mozley noted that the Old Testament evidence on divine suffering is ambiguous because of two aspects of the Hebrew mind.[17] First, the Hebrews generally made a radical distinction between God and the world. This attitude is reflected in Heschel's paraphrase of Isaiah given above. Second, the Hebrew mind was basically nonspeculative. The Hebrews complemented their emphasis on divine transcendence with bold, anthropopathic descriptions of God. There does not seem to be any significant change in this practice throughout their history. From the Pentateuch to the post-exilic Prophets, God is characterized by human feelings. Jewish theology, like later Christian theology, was influenced by Greek philosophy, and the living God of the Hebrews became the impersonal absolute. Such a transition is especially clear in the thought of Philo of Alexandria.[18]

Many of the emphases in the Hebrew understanding of God are preserved in the New Testament. Although proponents of divine suffering generally argue that the entire message of the New Testament directly or indirectly supports their claim, a few examples must suffice here. Many of these arguments focus on the life, ministry, death, and resurrection of Christ. The incarnation is taken as

---

[15]Ibid., 56.

[16]Harold Knight, *The Hebrew Prophetic Consciousness* (London: Lutterworth Press, 1947) 138.

[17]Mozley, *The Impassibility of God*, 1-4.

[18]T. E. Pollard, "The Impassibility of God," *Scottish Journal of Theology* 8 (December 1955): 355-56.

clear evidence of God's love and concern for humanity. The explicit statement "God is love" in 1 John 4:8 as well as passages such as John 3:16 are often cited. Some use the Pauline concept of *kenosis* (self-emptying) in Philippians 2:5-11 as additional support for divine suffering. Jesus' teaching on the fatherhood of God also lends plausibility to divine passibility. For example, R. S. Franks commented that "the fundamental New Testament doctrine of God's Fatherhood suggests the very reverse of His impassibility."[19] Jesus' ministry was characterized by identification with the poor, oppressed, outcast, and alienated of society. This identification mirrors the identification of Yahweh with the Hebrews.

Probably the key evidence for divine suffering in the New Testament is the passion of Christ. Adherents of divine suffering avoid a simplistic projection of Christ's agony onto the character of God, but many see the passion of Christ as a significant, perhaps the ultimate sign of God's pain. C. A. Dinsmore, for example, suggests "there was a cross in the heart of God before there was one planted on the green hill outside of Jerusalem. And now that the cross of wood has been taken down, the one in the heart of God abides, and it will remain so long as there is one sinful soul for whom to suffer."[20] The relationship between God's passion and Christ's passion demands careful explanation, which can be done only within the context of trinitarian and christological reflection. As we will see shortly, several early theologians argued that Christ's human nature, but not his divine nature, suffered.

Despite the emphasis on divine passion in the Bible, early Christian theologians gradually agreed on divine impassibility as the orthodox position. This development has been the target of most proponents of divine passibility, who generally agree that the main culprit responsible for the shift from passibility to impassibility is Greek metaphysics. Greek philosophers (e.g., Plato, Ar-

---

[19]R. S. Franks, "Passibility and Impassibility," in James Hastings, ed., *Encyclopaedia of Religion and Ethics* 9 (New York: Charles Scribner's Sons, 1928) 658.

[20]Charles Allen Dinsmore, *Atonement in Literature and Life* (Boston: Houghton, Mifflin, and Company, 1906) 232-33.

istotle, Parmenides, the Stoics) developed an understanding of deity as immutable, self-sufficient, impassible, and static. Christian theologians eventually used these philosophical categories to describe God, even though this usually led to a distortion of God's nature. God appeared more and more like Aristotle's unmoved mover, for example, rather than the passionate, dynamic Yahweh of biblical faith. Only within the last couple of centuries has there been a genuine recovery of the biblical emphasis on divine suffering. Rather than attempt a systematic review of the history of the doctrine of impassibility, I will give several examples of theological opinion in the course of Christian history.[21]

Some early theologians such as Ignatius and Irenaeus still occasionally link Christ's passion with God's passion, but they usually go on to rule out suffering as a legitimate divine attribute. They adhere to the paradoxical position that God could not suffer except in Christ. Referring to Christ in his letter to the Romans (6.3), Ignatius says, "Let me imitate the Passion of my God"; but in his letter to Polycarp (3.2), he describes God as "the Timeless, the Unseen, the One who became visible for our sakes, who was beyond touch and passion, yet who for our sakes became subject to suffering, and endured everything for us."[22] Irenaeus also could describe Christ as impassible yet capable of suffering in the incarnate state (*Against Heresies* 3,16.6). The apologists frequently agreed with the Greeks that emotions are not fitting for deity. Immutability and impassibility were increasingly linked together. D. M. Baillie once noted that in these early centuries divine impassibility may have been assumed rather than being the conclusion of an argument.[23] As the *via negativa* and Neoplatonic thought exercised more influence in doctrinal development, God's transcendence was further accentuated and anthropopathic language was summarily

---

[21]Mozley, *The Impassibility of God*, is the definitive study of the topic through the first quarter of this century.

[22]Cyril C. Richardson, ed., *Early Christian Fathers* (*The Library of Christian Classics, Volume 1*) (Philadelphia: Westminster Press, 1953) 105, 118-19.

[23]Pollard, "The Impassibility of God," 357.

dismissed. Very early theologians began to distinguish between Christ's divine and human natures: his divine nature was impassible and his human nature was passible.

The patripassianist controversy of the third century helped crystallize the impassibility position. The patripassianists suggested that the Father (*pater*) suffered (*passio*) in the crucifixion and death of the Son. When theologians such as Praxeas, Noetus, and Sabellius developed their modalistic monarchian Christology, their views were condemned as heretical.[24] In general they argued so forcefully for the unity of God (monarchianism) that they rejected any distinctions among the three members of the Trinity. The apex of this was the implication that God suffered and died on the cross with the Son. The patripassianists sought to guarantee the full deity of Christ, but orthodox Christians did not want the Father to suffer. The orthodox theologians insisted on strict trinitarian distinctions and on removing any passibility from the Father. Tertullian, for example, argued against Praxeas that God the Father did not experience suffering (*passio*) or sympathy (*compassio*) with the Son.[25] Mozley's judgment is that "Tertullian's description of the character of the divine feelings reads like a Christianized version of the Stoic exaltation" of *apatheia*.[26] The typical Greek ranking of reason above emotion or passion also had considerable influence. The Alexandrian theologians (e.g., Clement, Origen) reinforced this denial of divine passibility with their use of the *via negativa* and allegorical exegesis. Anthropopathic descriptions must not be taken literally; they must contain some deeper, spiritual meaning. According to Mozley, one of the Alexandrian theologians, Gregory Thaumaturgus, composed the only monograph in Christian history before the nineteenth century devoted to the topic of impassibility.[27] Gregory argues that God cannot experience a conflict

---

[24]Jaroslav Pelikan, *The Emergence of the Catholic Tradition (100-600)* (Chicago: University of Chicago Press, 1971) 176-80.

[25]Pollard, "The Impassibility of God," 358, notes that Tertullian was the first to argue for the impassibility of the divine nature in Christ.

[26]Mozley, *The Impassibility of God*, 38.

[27]Ibid., viii.

between his will and his nature because of the unity of his character. God is impassible, yet aware of human suffering and concerned to overcome that suffering.[28]

The impassibility doctrine was so widely assumed in early Christian history that quite often the orthodox and their opponents would agree on divine impassibility while disagreeing on other issues. In the Arian controversy, for example, both Arius and Athanasius assumed that God was incapable of suffering. The other christological and trinitarian controversies that led up to the confession of Chalcedon in A. D. 451 did not entail debate on impassibility. The monophysites, however, argued so strongly for the unity of divinity and humanity in Christ (one *physis* or nature) after the Incarnation that many orthodox feared divine passibility would be required. Divine passibility was again explicitly denied during the theopaschite controversy of the sixth century. Several Scythian monks proposed that one of the Trinity suffered, but this was rejected as heretical.[29]

Augustine and most of the scholastic theologians upheld the impassibility tradition. Augustine defined *passio* as "a commotion of the mind contrary to reason" and therefore inappropriate for God.[30] Anthropopathic language was included in the Bible because of the limitations of human language and understanding. Although Augustine's influence was strong on this topic (as on many others in the Middle Ages), the paradox of a loving and impassible God remained. Anselm asked:

> But again, how art thou at once compassionate and impassible? For if thou art impassible, thou canst not suffer with others, and if thou canst not suffer with others, thy heart is not wretched out of sympathy for the wretched—but this is what being compassionate means. Yet if thou are not compassionate, whence does such great consolation come to the wretched?[31]

---

[28]Ibid., 63-72.

[29]Pelikan, *Emergence of the Catholic Tradition*, 270-71.

[30]Saint Augustine, *The City of God*, trans. Marcus Dods (New York: Random House, 1950) 263.

[31]Eugene R. Fairweather, ed., *A Scholastic Miscellany: Anselm to Ockham* (New York: Macmillan, 1970) 77.

Anselm concluded that God is impassible and insisted that he *appears* compassionate to us; however, his essence is not marked by any real emotion. In a similar vein, Thomas Aquinas upholds the impassibility tradition. God is *actus purus* and cannot experience any change, contingency, or emotion. God can love mankind, but without any passion.

The Protestant Reformers did not bring about any dramatic shift on the impassibility issue. Except for the Socinians and some Anabaptists, impassibility remained the consensus.[32] The only major reformer who seemed receptive at all to divine passibility was Martin Luther. Luther's doctrine of *communicatio idiomatum* stressed the reciprocity of the divine and human natures and the sharing of attributes. If Christ suffered, then logically God suffered.[33] Overall, though, impassibility was regnant among the Reformers and the Protestant Scholastics. Divine impassibility is explicitly upheld in the Thirty-nine Articles of the Church of England (art. 1) and the Westminster Confession (ch. 2).

In the nineteenth and twentieth centuries divine impassibility has received increasing criticism. Reflecting on the modern period in general, Mozley noted the "occasional" character of the reaction against impassibility: many modern writers fail to treat the subject rigorously, even though there has been a basic shift in opinion.[34] Mozley then isolates two major influences on this shift—metaphysics and natural science. (1) Regarding metaphysics, Mozley cites the philosophy of Lotze, the reaction against Hegelianism, and the attractiveness of a finite God (e.g., William James, James Ward, A. S. Pringle-Pattison). (2) Natural science indirectly influenced acceptance of divine passibility through the popularity of the new evolutionary world view. Theists argued that God is immanent in

---

[32]Mozley, *The Impassibility of God*, 119.

[33]Paul Althaus, *The Theology of Martin Luther*, trans. Robert C. Schultz (Philadelphia: Fortress Press, 1966) 197, argues that Luther holds to deipassionism rather than patripassianism; that is, God rather than the Father suffered.

[34]Mozley, *The Impassibility of God*, 124.

the evolutionary struggle. As a result of these influences and others, by the end of the nineteenth century divine passibility was increasingly acceptable as a theological opinion. For the period 1866-1926 Mozley lists the following as proponents of divine suffering: Bishop Martensen, A. J. Mason, W. N. Clarke, Horace Bushnell, Principal Simon, Vincent Tymms, A. M. Fairbairn, G. B. Stevens, C. A. Dinsmore, Campbell Morgan, S. A. McDowell, Douglas White, Canon Storr, C. E. Rolt, Canon Streeter, G. A. Studdert-Kennedy, Archbishop D'Arcy, Miss Dougall, William Temple, E. L. Strong, and Maldwyn Hughes.

On into the twentieth century divine passibility was quite frequently affirmed, although I suggested earlier that most were satisfied to assert the position without explaining the reasons for it. The challenge to divine impassibility has correctly been designated "one of the most striking developments in theology today," representing a "structural shift in the Christian mind."[35] Writing in 1977, S. Paul Schilling noted that in his research he encountered at least forty-two theologians since 1926 who have criticized divine impassibility and/or affirmed divine passibility.[36] Further, this shift away from the traditional position cuts across geographical and denominational lines.

Since the major purpose of this study is to examine selected proponents of divine passion, my concern here is simply to sketch some of the general factors in the twentieth century that have reinforced this shift. Daniel Day Williams helpfully proposed three such factors as the basic ones.[37] (1) Developments in contemporary metaphysics have encouraged the divine-passion position. He cites in particular the influence of Charles Hartshorne, Edgar Brightman, F. R. Tennant, and A. N. Whitehead. Certainly the emphasis of process theologians on the dynamic, active involvement of God in human history makes them natural supporters of divine pas-

---

[35]Daniel Day Williams, *What Present Day Theologians Are Thinking*, 3d ed. (New York: Harper & Row, 1967) 171-72.

[36]Schilling, *God and Human Anguish*, 251.

[37]Williams, *What Present Day Theologians Are Thinking*, 172-75.

sion. Daniel Day Williams has been selected for intensive examination in this study as an example of the process perspective. (2)
The biblical-theology movement, which flourished after World War
II, understood God as an active participant in history. The He-
braic-Christian God is a temporal being who responds to developments in time. These writers frequently contrast this view of God
with the typical view of God as eternal and static that infiltrated
early Christian theology.[38] The consequent de-Hellenization of orthodox theology results in criticism of impassibility. Many theologians outside of the biblical-theology movement have accepted
their arguments in this area. (3) Contemporary understandings of
the atonement have further accentuated belief in the divine passion. Examination of the cross as the decisive action of God in history reverses the normal procedure of orthodox theology.
Theologians usually determined their view of divinity and attempted to fit the passion of Christ into that scheme. Recent theologians have tried to be more Christocentric in their orientation,
taking the passion of Christ as the clue to the passion of God. In
sum, these factors and others have contributed to the growing
consensus about divine suffering in the twentieth century.

IS GOD PASSIONATE OR PASSIONLESS?
THE CONTEMPORARY DEBATE

Although many contemporary theologians agree that God suffers in some way, many others would still resist such a character-
ization of God. Before turning to an examination of selected
proponents of divine passibility, I perhaps should survey briefly
some of the arguments for and against divine passion. These arguments will not be expanded here, but will serve simply to intro-
duce several facets of the debate.

First, there are several reasons why divine impassibility is still
asserted by some. Several lists are offered here as examples. After
tracing the history of divine impassibility through the early twen-

---

[38]Brevard S. Childs, *Biblical Theology in Crisis* (Philadelphia: Westminster Press, 1970) 44-47.

tieth century, J. K. Mozley noted three reasons why it is still viable. (1) Divine transcendence is better preserved with divine impassibility than passibility. God's nature precludes any points of contact with human nature or feelings. (2) The "life of God is a blessed life, and, as such, happy with the perfection of happiness."[39] If God suffered with human suffering, his happiness would be disturbed. (3) The fear of anthropomorphism prohibited the use of anthropomorphic or anthropopathic descriptions of God. To take such descriptions of God too literally would detract from God's deity.

A similar but fuller list of objections to divine passion was proposed by Baron Friedrich von Hügel, a German Roman Catholic theologian, in a lecture in 1921. (1) "Suffering is intrinsically evil."[40] Baron von Hügel notes that proponents of divine suffering always have God transform the suffering into joy because they implicitly agree that suffering is evil. They do not really mean that God suffers; for them God must ultimately experience joy. (2) Although suffering and sin are not identical, they are so intimately linked together in the Bible that to attribute one to God might imply the other. (3) Perfect freedom excludes choice, and divine perfection must necessitate perfect freedom. Human beings may experience freedom as a choice between good and evil, but the highest freedom is to do the good spontaneously and totally. If God had freedom of choice, then he might suffer. (4) Divine otherness is essential to true religion. Humanity may want a God who sympathizes with its misery, but its deepest need is for the joy God can offer. Baron von Hügel argues that God can sympathize with mankind without suffering. "Sympathy, yes, indeed, overflowing Sympathy—a Sympathy which we cannot succeed in picturing vividly without drawing upon our own experiences of ourselves, where sympathy and suffering are so closely intertwined; but no Suffering in God; and Suffering, indeed overflowing suffering in Christ, but as man, not as God."[41] (5) True religion requires a to-

---

[39]Mozley, *The Impassibility of God*, 172.

[40]Baron Friedrich von Hügel, *Essays and Addresses on the Philosophy of Religion (Second Series)* (London: J. M. Dent & Sons, 1926) 199.

[41]Ibid., 205.

tally transcendent God whose experience is undisturbed joy. For the baron, "God is that Perfect Love, Unmixed Joy, Entire Delectation" untouched by genuine suffering.[42] God may sympathize with us, but he may not suffer.

H. Wheeler Robinson supported divine suffering, but he listed three possible philosophical objections to divine passibility.[43] (1) Suffering usually involves frustration and limitation, yet God could not be frustrated. (2) Divine suffering would entangle God in time; such a God would not be able to satisfy mankind's religious needs. (3) A suffering God is the result of the projection of human personality onto God. God would be inferior to the Absolute of philosophical thought.

Although he also supports divine suffering, S. Paul Schilling briefly lists five "overlapping propositions" held by supporters of impassibility.[44] (1) Divine transcendence precludes any finite limitations for God. (2) God must be absolute and eternal, as the Greeks have demonstrated. (3) God's "perfect blessedness" allows sympathy for the human situation, but real suffering is excluded. (4) Biblical texts depicting God suffering are figurative, and only the human nature of Christ suffered. (5) Religious consciousness demands an omnipotent, omniscient God who commands adoration, not a suffering God.

Several arguments have been proposed *for* divine passion. Several lists of such arguments are given here as examples. J. K. Mozley noted three motives prompting the propassibility position.[45] (1) God as love is a central theme in the Christian faith. To love necessitates the possibility of suffering; otherwise God would be indifferent and unloving. (2) Divine immanence must complement divine transcendence. If God is actively engaged in the world, he must be sensitive to its suffering. (3) The cross points back to the

---

[42]Ibid., 208.

[43]H. Wheeler Robinson, *Suffering, Human and Divine* (New York: Macmillan, 1939) 146-48.

[44]Schilling, *God and Human Anguish*, 251.

[45]Mozley, *The Impassibility of God*, 175-77.

heart of God and reveals God's eternal nature. In more technical terms, Christology (especially soteriology) becomes definitive of theology.

H. Wheeler Robinson offered several reasons for divine suffering, but here I will note only how he responded to the three objections to divine suffering mentioned above.[46] (1) God does not experience physical suffering as men do, though he does undergo spiritual suffering or a suffering of moral sympathy. God can limit himself voluntarily rather than being limited by external realities. (2) Time must not be devalued in contrast with eternity; it must mean something to God and add something to his experience. (3) Robinson insists that a dynamic, temporal God is more adequate to the needs of the religious consciousness than the Absolute of the philosophers.

Slightly different reasons for the passion of God were offered by T. E. Pollard as he criticized divine impassibility.[47] (1) To argue that God does not suffer would entail rewriting the Bible or assuming the descriptions of God are primitive anthropomorphisms. The Bible consistently stresses the personal character of God, which includes the emotive dimension. Pollard criticizes early theologians for allowing Greek philosophy to depersonalize God. In attempting to say God is more than personal, these theologians actually used subpersonal rather than suprapersonal categories. (2) The incarnation of God in Jesus is not a real incarnation if God is impassible. He argues that all divine attributes apply to the entire Godhead. If God is impassible, then, the impassible Son is incarnate in Jesus. In that case a docetic Christology results, even though the New Testament clearly notes Jesus' human feelings. Also, Pollard rejects the argument that only the human nature of Christ suffered by pointing to the confession of Chalcedon, which stressed the indivisibility of his two natures. (3) Divine impassibility logically means that the work of Christ "is merely a human work, and His death on the cross is the death of man and not the death of a Son of God." Christ's death must be both divine and human if it is

---

[46]Robinson, *Suffering, Human and Divine*, 148-55.

[47]Pollard, "The Impassibility of God," 360-64.

to be efficacious for mankind. Pollard concludes his essay by noting that divine impassibility ultimately rejects the personality of
God. He also insists that Baron von Hügel's distinction between
divine sympathy and suffering does not hold up, for "if we can as-
cribe *compassio* to God there is no reason why we should not as-
cribe *passio* to Him as well."[48]

S. Paul Schilling offers several reasons for his support of divine
suffering.[49] (1) Impassibility theologians work with an a priori
judgment about divine perfection rather than examining concrete
experience. Consequently, God is seen as the absolute, unrelated
supreme being rather than as a loving, suffering God. (2) The Bible
stresses the immanence of God as well as transcendence. (3) The
incarnation, life, and death of Jesus "must manifest central truth
regarding the life and character of God. Then the cross speaks to
us decisively of the suffering love of God himself."[50] (4) The two-
natures Christology of Chalcedon and earlier creeds should not be
used to distinguish artificially between the human suffering of
Christ and the divine nature's impassibility. (5) If God does not
suffer, he is not love. True love demands the ability to suffer. (6)
The religious consciousness desires a God who knows human dis-
tress. Human sufferers are not consoled by an absolute, passionless God.

The mere listing of these arguments for and against divine passion is not intended as a substitute for critical discussion of the issue. Rather, the purpose has been to give the reader some overview
of the debate.

THE NEW PATRIPASSIANISTS?

The following chapters are devoted to the analysis of six contemporary theologians who favor divine passion: Jürgen Molt-

---

[48]Ibid., 363, notes that Baron von Hügel uses the *passio/compassio* distinction to maintain impassibility, while Tertullian rejected such a distinction in his attack on the patripassianists.

[49]Schilling, *God and Human Anguish*, 252-56.

[50]Ibid., 253.

mann, James Cone, Geddes MacGregor, Kazoh Kitamori, Daniel Day Williams, and Jung Lee. Perhaps these men can be called, without too much distortion, the new patripassianists. Only one of the six (MacGregor) would explicitly allow the use of that label, and several disavow it. Certainly most would not agree with the exact formulation of the patripassianist position in the third century. They would insist on stronger trinitarian distinctions than the old patripassianists, yet in general they do agree that God suffers.

These six were chosen for intensive study for a variety of reasons. First, each has made the passion of God a crucial theme in his theology. As noted earlier, Schilling has compiled a list of forty-two theologians who have supported divine passibility in the last half century. In many ways the reaction against impassibility is still "occasional," to use Mozley's term, because many of these theologians do not make the issue central to their program. These six have not all written works totally devoted to divine passion, but they have singled out the theme for significant attention.

Second, all six have been prominent since World War II and reflect theological concerns for this half of the twentieth century. Kitamori's *Theology of the Pain of God*, published in 1946, is the oldest work treated here. The choice of the postwar time frame is somewhat arbitrary since Mozley's survey only reached up to 1926. The period 1926-1946 saw a few articles and books on the subject, but the debate was not as intense as earlier in the century. Baron von Hügel's essay, discussed earlier, provoked Francis J. McConnell's *Is God Limited?*[51] McConnell argued for divine passibility by insisting that suffering would not limit God. In 1928 B. R. Brasnett published *The Suffering of the Impassible God* in which he argued that an impassible God could lay aside his impassibility and freely accept suffering.[52] H. Wheeler Robinson argued for divine suffering primarily on exegetical grounds in *Suffering, Human and Divine*.[53] Ki-

---

[51]Francis J. McConnell, *Is God Limited?* (London: Williams and Norgate, 1924).

[52]Bertrand R. Brasnett, *The Suffering of the Impassible God* (London: S. P. C. K. Press, 1928).

[53]Robinson, *Suffering, Human and Divine*.

tamori's work in 1946, *Theology of the Pain of God*, signaled a new interest in divine suffering.

Third, these six were chosen to represent a variety of rationales for divine passion. One unusual aspect of the propassibility movement is that so many theologians have reached the same conclusion from a wide range of starting points. Jürgen Moltmann uses a strongly christological orientation and the resources of the theology-of-hope movement to support divine passion. He combines an interest in reviving Luther's *theologia crucis* with political activism. For Moltmann, Christ's cry of Godforsakenness on the cross (Mark 15:34) must be the catalyst for a truly Christian understanding of God. He develops an eschatological panentheism as the context for this activity of the "crucified God." His eschatological orientation produces a political hermeneutic of the Gospel designed to spark Christian action against oppression and injustice. James Cone writes on behalf of the oppressed minorities, especially American blacks, and argues that the God who suffers with them is also the God who liberates them. For Cone, the crucifixion-resurrection of Jesus is a universal liberation event efficacious for all the oppressed of the world. Geddes MacGregor bases his propassibility conclusion on a kenotic understanding of God. Instead of restricting the self-limitation to the Son, MacGregor argues that the totality of God is self-emptying. For MacGregor, "God is love" (1 John 4:8) stands as the starting point for Christian theology. He criticizes traditional Christianity for succumbing to the idolatry of power or "dynamolatry." Kazoh Kitamori understands the pain of God to be the result of a struggle between divine love and divine wrath. God's pain arises from his loving the objects of his wrath, sinners. Kitamori's perspective is heavily influenced by his Lutheran theology of the cross. In addition, Kitamori tries to develop a Japanese understanding of the Christian faith that can avoid the distortions of Greek metaphysics. Daniel Day Williams develops a doctrine of divine sensitivity in light of his process theology and the fact of divine love. God is both vulnerable to the world's misery yet invulnerable to ultimate defeat. Jung Lee proposes divine empathy as central to God's character because of divine love and the influence of the *I ching*. According to him, change is more basic to the universe and to God than traditional Western theology has recognized.

Fourth, these six were chosen to reflect a variety of geographic, ethnic, and denominational backgrounds. All six are Protestant, but they represent a wide range of theological traditions. Two come from the so-called "younger" churches of the Third World (Kitamori, Lee), while one comes from an American minority group (Cone). Some Roman Catholic and Eastern Orthodox theologians have been sympathetic to divine passibility, but the Protestants have generally been more vocal on the issue.[54] The backgrounds represented are German Lutheran (Moltmann), American black Methodist (Cone), American Presbyterian (MacGregor), Japanese Lutheran (Kitamori), American Congregationalist (Williams), and Korean Methodist (Lee).

Now that the major issue for our study has been suggested and the cast of characters has been introduced, the remainder of the study will focus on critical analysis of these six theologians. Although these six theologians could be studied independently and the next six chapters could be read in any order, the order of presentation reflects some progression of thought. The first three theologians (Moltmann, Cone, MacGregor) are relatively better known to most students of contemporary theology, and they frequently draw on themes prominent in mainstream Western theology. Moltmann's theology of hope represents an attempt to highlight eschatology while underscoring the need for social action. Much of the liberation theology of Europe and the Americas, represented here by Cone's black theology, draws consciously from Moltmann's interest in political theology. MacGregor is treated next because his clearest critique of the impassibility tradition was based on the *kenosis* theme in Paul's letter to the Philippians and John's

---

[54]Among Roman Catholics, see Hans Küng, *On Being a Christian*, trans. Edward Quinn (New York: Pocket Books, 1978) 428-36. Among Eastern Orthodox theologians, Nicolas Berdyaev is probably the best example. See Charles Hartshorne, "Whitehead and Berdyaev: Is There Tragedy in God?" *Journal of Religion* 37 (April 1957): 71-84. See also Jürgen Moltmann, *The Trinity and the Kingdom: The Doctrine of God*, trans. Margaret Kohl (San Francisco: Harper & Row, 1981) 42-47.

definition of God as love (1 John 4:8). Although some of Mac-
Gregor's most recent work draws on non-Western sources, our
study will focus on his theology of kenotic love. The last three authors (Kitamori, Williams, Lee) are grouped together because they
reflect more self-conscious attempts to go beyond the traditional
Western theism. Williams, as a process theologian, critiques the
impassibility tradition philosophically and exegetically. Kitamori
represents a Third-World perspective that draws primarily from the
Japanese context. Lee, a Korean, is treated last because he draws
from process theology as well as his Asian heritage.

The overall perspective of this book is a critical appreciation for
the divine-suffering perspective. The affirmation of divine suffering seems to be closer to the deepest insights of the Christian faith
than does the impassibility perspective. Although I am receptive
to the insights of these six theologians, I intend to analyze their positions critically. Each of these six concludes that God suffers, but
the articulation of each position may not be equally valid. Each
theologian will be analyzed independently, and the concluding
chapter will include some general concerns about these contemporary proponents of divine passion.

No attempt will be made to offer a full-blown proposal about
divine suffering. Certainly interacting with these six theologians
and others of a similar orientation would prepare the way for such
a constructive move. Again, the final chapter will offer some suggestions about the direction such a proposal could go.

Chapter Two

Jürgen Moltmann:
The Crucified God

In 1964 Jürgen Moltmann, a young German theologian, captured international attention with the publication of *Theology of Hope*.[1] He was acknowledged quickly as one of the leading figures in the "theology of hope" movement in Europe and North America. In

---

[1]In this chapter the following abbreviations are used for Moltmann's major works:

CPS   *The Church in the Power of the Spirit: A Contribution to Messianic Ecclesiology*, trans. Margaret Kohl (New York: Harper & Row, 1977)

CG   *The Crucified God: The Cross of Christ as the Foundation and Criticism of Christian Theology*, trans. R. A. Wilson and John Bowden (New York: Harper & Row, 1974)

EH   *The Experiment Hope*, ed. M. Douglas Meeks (Philadelphia: Fortress Press, 1975)

FOH   *The Future of Hope: Theology as Eschatology*, ed. Frederick Herzog (New York: Herder and Herder, 1970)

HP   *Hope and Planning*, trans. Margaret Clarkson (New York: Harper & Row, 1971)

PL   *The Passion for Life: A Messianic Lifestyle*, trans. M. Douglas Meeks (Philadelphia: Fortress Press, 1978)

RRF   *Religion, Revolution, and the Future*, trans. M. Douglas Meeks (New York: Charles Scribner's Sons, 1969)

TH   *Theology of Hope: On the Ground and Implications of a Christian Eschatology*, trans. James W. Leitch (London: SCM Press, 1967)

Two articles duplicate much of the material in *CG* and are not cited when the same emphasis appears in *CG*: "The 'Crucified God': A Trinitarian Theology of the Cross," *Interpretation* 26 (July 1972): 278-99; "The Crucified God," *Theology Today* 31 (April 1974): 6-18.

this chapter my concern is to examine Moltmann's understanding of God, especially God's relationship to the problem of suffering. Although Moltmann's theology is multifaceted, my focus will be directed primarily to his theodicy and his affirmation of divine suffering. Moltmann has not devoted any one book exclusively to divine suffering, but it is a theme that permeates his most recent writing.

HUMAN SUFFERING
AND THE GOD OF HOPE

The emergence of several eschatological theologies in the last two decades is one of the most unusual developments in recent theological history. Christians have always been interested in the future and eschatology (i.e., the study of last things), but interest has risen and fallen several times in the nearly two thousand years of Christian history. Earlier in this century eschatology was a hotly debated topic because of the revival of the apocalypse in biblical studies, especially through the work of Johannes Weiss and Albert Schweitzer.[2] Only in the 1960s, however, did any major systematic theologians take eschatology as the dominant factor in their theological reflection. The theology-of-hope movement—represented by figures such as Moltmann, Wolfhart Pannenberg, Johannes B. Metz, Gerhard Sauter, and Carl Braaten—was convinced that God is preeminently the "God of hope" (Romans 15:13) who calls Christians to a future full of possibilities and promise.[3] These theologians are concerned about several interrelated issues and represent a "common front," though they do not have a totally unified

---

[2]See Johannes Weiss, *Jesus' Proclamation of the Kingdom of God*, trans. and ed. Richard H. Hiers and David L. Holland (Philadelphia: Fortress Press, 1971) and Albert Schweitzer, *The Quest of the Historical Jesus*, trans. W. Montgomery (New York: Macmillan, 1961).

[3]For a general introduction to the movement, see Walter H. Capps, ed., *The Future of Hope* (Philadelphia: Fortress Press, 1970) and Capps, *Time Invades the Cathedral: Tensions in the School of Hope* (Philadelphia: Fortress Press, 1972).

theological program.[4] Some have seen the popularity of eschato-logical theology as a logical reaction to the radical theology of the 1960s. The *New York Times* front-page headline for 24 March 1968 read: " 'God is Dead' Doctrine Is Losing Ground to the 'Theology of Hope.' " The background for eschatological theology, as we shall see shortly, is more complex than this.

Because the theology-of-hope movement is a rather loose school of thought, it is extremely difficult to note all of the factors leading to its appearance. Christopher Morse, writing about Moltmann, cites four primary influences, which will serve to give a general introduction to the movement.[5] First, Morse notes that both Karl Barth and Rudolf Bultmann tried to appropriate the apocalyptic research of Weiss and Schweitzer. Moltmann is highly critical of their proposals; therefore, his theology is a fresh effort to take eschatology seriously. Second, the renaissance of the apocalypse in biblical studies in the last few years has influenced the eschatological theologians.[6] These theologians have tried to draw out the systematic implications of eschatology for the Christian faith. Third, the philosophy of Ernst Bloch and the Christian-Marxist dialogue raised issues central to the eschatological theologians. Moltmann, perhaps more than other theologian of hope, has been influenced by the Marxist philosopher Bloch, whose major work is *Daz Prinzip Hoffnung* (*The Hope Principle*). Although critical of some aspects of Bloch's thought, Moltmann is receptive to Bloch's stress on the future. Moltmann interacted with other Marxists in the Christian-Marxist dialogue that flourished until the Soviet repression of the

---

[4]Jürgen Moltmann, "The Theology of Hope Today," *The Critic* 26 (1968): 22.

[5]Christopher Morse, *The Logic of Promise in Moltmann's Theology* (Philadelphia: Fortress Press, 1979) 6-16. See another list of influences in Capps, *Future of Hope*, 4-19. For a fuller account of the influences on Moltmann in particular, see M. Douglas Meeks, *Origins of the Theology of Hope* (Philadelphia: Fortress Press, 1974).

[6]See the excellent summary in E. Frank Tupper, "The Revival of Apocalyptic in Biblical and Theological Studies," *Review and Expositor* 72 (Summer 1975): 279-304.

Dubcek government in Czechoslovakia. Fourth, the theology-of-hope movement was spurred by the general cultural concern with the future. Moltmann, for example, sees the interest in the future as a point of contact between the contemporary secular mind and biblical thought. Other theological, philosophical, biblical, and cultural influences have been operative in the theology of hope, but the four listed are representative.

One of the more unusual results of eschatological theology has been a widespread concern for liberation, revolution, and political theologies.[7] Many times in Christian history eschatological thought has been speculative and otherworldly to such an extent that it has been divorced from present human misery. Indeed, there is a prevailing belief that concern for the future (e.g., return of Christ, heaven, and hell) precludes human action to alleviate suffering in the present. Although this belief could be disproved in other contexts, the theology of hope has not ignored this world for the sake of another transcendent future world. Moltmann's position on eschatological ethics is typical: he consistently argues that an understanding of God's promise for the future should prompt Christian action in the present. He proposes, for example, that Christians must develop a "political hermeneutic of the gospel" in order to understand it correctly (*RRF* 83-107). The eschatological theologians, in other words, are not suggesting a new version of the pie-in-the-sky solution to the problem of human suffering. The God of hope provides *real hope* and concern for the present.

Having completed this general introduction to the concerns of the eschatological theologians, we need to focus in a preliminary way on Moltmann's program, particularly on the relationship of hope and suffering. Moltmann clearly sees theodicy as a central concern for the Christian faith. "Today it is again recognized that Christian theology has its broadest and most controversial relationship to the world within the horizon of the question of theodicy" (*HP* 52). Like other theologians of hope, Moltmann insists

---

[7]Another theologian of hope who links the suffering of God and political activism is Rubem A. Alves, *A Theology of Human Hope* (New York: Corpus Books, 1969) esp. 114-32.

that a viable Christian theology and theodicy can be articulated within an eschatological context. Eschatology should not be an irrelevant appendix to the Christian faith that is of concern only to fanatical, revolutionary sects. Eschatology is the doctrine of Christian hope, including both the object hoped for and the hope generated by the object (*TH* 16). Its concern is only partially with the future. Moltmann is especially sensitive to the charge that eschatology and Christian activism are mutually exclusive.

> Hope finds in Christ not only a consolation *in* suffering, but also the protest of the divine promise *against* suffering. . . . That is why faith, wherever it develops into hope, causes not rest but unrest, not patience but impatience. It does not calm the unquiet heart, but is itself this unquiet heart in man. Those who hope in Christ can no longer put up with reality as it is, but begin to suffer under it, to contradict it. Peace with God means conflict with the world, for the goad of the promised future stabs inexorably into the flesh of every unfulfilled present (*TH* 21).

The consolation the Christian feels in the midst of suffering derives primarily from the knowledge of the "crucified God" suffering with mankind. Christians are also encouraged, however, to work politically to create a freer and more humane society now (*RRF* 118-22).

Moltmann recognizes the real danger of hopelessness in the twentieth century. Such hopelessness can take two forms: presumption and despair (*TH* 22-26). Presumption is the attitude that expectations will be fulfilled according to a human timetable. Despair is the attitude that hopes will not be fulfilled in any way in human history. Presumption may have been a serious threat to the Christian faith in the nineteenth century, but despair is more typical of the twentieth century; in short, Prometheus has been replaced by Sisyphus. Rather than being too utopian in outlook, contemporary man tends to be resigned to "the worst of all utopias, the utopia of the *status quo*" (*TH* 23). Contemporary Christians too readily assume that human suffering and the condition of the world are irreparable short of the *eschaton*. Christian hope, argues Moltmann, is more realistic than either despair or presumption and can help destroy these two perversions of hope. Christians can participate in hope movements and liberation movements, but Christian hope "must oppose the vainglory in every movement filled with human hope for greater freedom and social justice" (*RRF* 121).

Although Moltmann gained prominence initially as a theologian of hope, his interests have diversified in the last decade or so. His three major theological works reveal the refinements and shifts of his thought. *Theology of Hope* (1964) epitomizes Moltmann's concern with eschatology. His Christology in this work focused on the resurrection of Christ, and he emphasized the role of Christians in modern society as the "Exodus church." *The Crucified God* (1972) focused on the crucifixion of Christ and developed the christological and trinitarian implications of the cross. Moltmann's emphasis on the suffering of God surfaces here most clearly; for that reason, it will be one of the central texts in our study. His continuing concern for the alleviation of human suffering is accented through proposals about the psychological and political liberation of mankind. *The Church in the Power of the Spirit* (1975) draws out the implications of the earlier works for his view of the church and the Spirit. He again tries to maintain a balance between the suffering of God and human action against injustice and oppression. He suggests, for example, that Christians must be consoled in suffering *and* offer resistance to it. "Without resistance, consolation in suffering can decline into a mere injunction to patience. But without consolation in suffering, resistance to suffering can lead to suffering being repressed, pushed aside so that in the end it actually increases" (*CPS* 113). In more recent works, such as *The Future of Creation, Experiences of God*, and *The Trinity and the Kingdom*, Moltmann has not made any significant new moves on the subject of theodicy. He consistently holds to the suffering of God as a valuable clue to a fully Christian theodicy. *The Crucified God* remains his primary contribution to the theodicy issue.

Although human suffering has been one of Jürgen Moltmann's concerns throughout his career, it has emerged in his latest writings as a basic component of his thought. So far Moltmann has not dedicated a systematic treatise to the theodicy issue, but the major outlines of his approach are becoming clear. He acknowledges that "human suffering is the central problem in most religions" (*CPS* 161), and he attempts to bring the resources of his eschatological understanding of the Christian faith to bear on the issue. He limits the scope of his effort by arguing that the fundamental form of the theodicy question for contemporary man is a political one (e.g., Auschwitz) rather than the traditional naturalistic one (e.g., the Lisbon earthquake of 1755) (*RRF* 205). Apparently the atrocities of "moral" evil have impressed Moltmann more forcefully than the tragedy of "natural" evil such as tornadoes, leukemia, and earthquakes. He frequently cites two examples of human suffering to illustrate the contemporary shape of the problem. In Elie Wiesel's *Night* two Jewish men and a boy are hanged by the Germans. As the boy dies a slow death, someone asks, "Where is God?" Wiesel responds, "Where is he? He is here. He is hanging there on the gallows" (*CG* 273-74). He also cites Ivan's offer in the *Brothers Karamazov* to give his admission ticket back to God because of the intense suffering of innocent children (*CG* 270). Moltmann's own experience as a prisoner of war in the last stages of World War II certainly accented this version of the theodicy problem for him.

Moltmann has begun to attack the theodicy issue, at least partially, because of its significance as an apologetic issue. He is convinced that Christian theology ought to address itself to other religions and ideologies and be a "theology of dialogue" (*EH* 12). A "crisis of relevance" in Christian faith further prompts the need for apologetics (*CG* 8-18). Certainly human suffering prompts many of the doubts about and attacks on the Christian faith in our time (*FOH* 3-6). Moltmann's response is basically double-pronged: an external apologetic to the protest atheism that uses suffering as a basis for denying God and an internal apologetic to the rigidly theistic view of God that makes a Christian theodicy impossible. Thus far the thrust of his discussion has been in the context of secularized Western culture. In his latest work, however, he also notes the apologetic value of his theodicy in relation to non-Christian religions (*CPS* 159-63).

In developing his theodicy, Moltmann's basic strategy has been to demonstrate that an authentically Christian understanding of God points to God suffering with us as we suffer. His insight into the "passion of God" is probably his major contribution to the contemporary discussion of the theodicy issue.[8] He recognizes that this emphasis will mean a revolution in our concept of God, but the new understanding will more adequately respond to the theodicy issue than can atheism or theism. The explicit basis for Moltmann's understanding of God is his interpretation of the cross of Christ as a fully trinitarian event: the passion of God is implied by the passion of Christ. "The cross of Christ then becomes the 'Christian theodicy'—a self-justification of God in which judgment and damnation are taken up by God himself, so that man may live" (HP 43). The goal of the rest of this chapter is to see how he moves from his Christology to his affirmation of God's suffering and then to examine the value of that claim for his theodicy.

THE PASSION OF CHRIST
AND THE CRUCIFIED GOD

In some ways Moltmann's Christology is traditional. For example, he uses the Chalcedonian categories of the humanity and deity of Jesus to organize some of his discussion (CG 87-98), and he follows the reformers' threefold office of Christ as a regulative principle (CPS 75-108). In addition, he is heavily indebted to Paul and Martin Luther for his general orientation, focusing on the death and resurrection of Christ. In his major treatise on Christology, The Crucified God, he frequently points to Luther's theologia crucis emphasis as central to authentic Christianity: "Theologia crucis is not a single chapter in theology, but the key signature for all Christian theology. . . . It is the point from which all theological statements which seek to be Christian are viewed (W. Loewenich)" (CG 72). Despite this formal similarity with the orthodox Christology, Moltmann is critical of some traditional understandings of Christ. For example, he argues that the doctrine of the two natures has been influenced unduly by the Greek philosophical tradition with its emphasis on the immutability and impassibility of God (CG 227-29).

---

[8]M. Douglas Meeks argues that "one objective of Moltmann's recent theology is to rehabilitate the word 'passion' for use in theology as well as everyday life in the church" (PL 16).

Moltmann's main concern in Christology is to understand the death and resurrection of Christ.[9] A serious treatment of the passion of Christ will lead to a more genuinely Christian understanding of God. He is most impressed with Jesus' cry of dereliction in Mark 15:34. "Jesus died crying out to God, 'My God, why hast thou forsaken me?' All Christian theology and all Christian life is basically an answer to the question which Jesus asked as he died" (*CG* 4). In *The Crucified God* Moltmann explores the Godforsakenness of Jesus in the context of a threefold account of the crucifixion (*CG* 126-53). (1) In relation to Jewish law, Jesus died as a blasphemer. (2) In relation to Roman authority, he died as a rebel. (3) In relation to God, he died an agonizing death marked by a deep sense of having been abandoned by God. Jesus' death was not the calm death of Socrates, the Zealot martyrs, the Stoics, or even later Christian martyrs. Rather, Jesus faced death with great apprehension and called out to an apparently absent God. Although Moltmann considers the quotation of Psalm 22:1 in Mark 15:34 to be a post-Easter interpretation by the church, it is "as near as possible to the historical reality of the death of Jesus" (*CG* 146-47). Moltmann sees the anguished cry of Jesus as a plea to God to demonstrate his righteousness and his deity. The torment is so great because of the prior intimate relationship of Father and Son. Looking at interpretations of Jesus' passion within the New Testament, Moltmann understands the sacrifice of the Son by the Father (Rom. 8:32, Gal. 2:20, John 3:16, Eph. 5:25) as an indication of God's active involvement in the death of Jesus. When Paul argues "God was in Christ" (2 Cor. 5:19), this implies that God himself suffered and died on the cross. "In the passion of the Son, the Father himself suffers the pains of abandonment. In the death of the Son, death comes upon God himself, and the Father suffers the death of his Son in his love for forsaken man. Consequently, what happened on the cross must

---

[9]Roland D. Zimany, "Moltmann's Crucified God," *Dialog* 16 (Winter 1977): 51, criticizes Moltmann for neglecting the life of Jesus and using too narrow a base on which to build his theology. Carl E. Braaten, "A Trinitarian Theology of the Cross," *The Journal of Religion* 56 (January 1976): 120, argues that Moltmann's theology of the cross is too dependent on Paul and reflects a reduction of the canon.

be understood as an event between God and the Son of God" (*CG* 192). The cry of Jesus from the cross is the true starting point for Christology and in turn for all of Christian theology.

In *The Church in the Power of the Spirit,* Moltmann again introduces the Godforsakenness of Christ, but this time the immediate context is the priestly office of Christ (*CPS* 85-98). Although Moltmann does not explicitly interact with the traditional atonement theories of Anselm, Abelard, Grotius, and others, he is concerned to show how Christ's death is significant for human life.[10] The three aspects of Christ's priestly work highlighted are liberation from the compulsion of sin, liberation from the idols of power, and liberation from Godforsakenness. In developing this third aspect, Moltmann again notes that the crucifixion of Jesus provides the best angle of vision into the nature of God. "Christ's surrender of himself to a Godforsaken death reveals the secret of the cross and with it the secret of God himself. It is the open secret of the Trinity" (*CPS* 95). Although Jesus experienced a descent into the hell of Godforsakenness, the cross demonstrates that God is for us and with us in our torment.

The centrality of the crucifixion of Jesus for Moltmann is not diminished when he turns to the Trinity's relation to eschatology (*CG* 256-66). Despite Moltmann's generally eschatological approach to theology, he will not let the future devalue the death and resurrection of Christ. Indeed, Moltmann is at great pains to show that *The Crucified God* does not involve a radical shift from the perspective of *Theology of Hope.* "*Theology of Hope* began with the *resurrection* of the crucified Christ, and I am now turning to look at the *cross* of the risen Christ" (*CG* 5). He is especially critical of attempts to understand Christ in a functional eschatological fashion which suggests that Christ will be superfluous when the Kingdom of God is established. His own interpretation of passages like 1 Corinthians 15:28 causes him to criticize the views of John Calvin, A. A. van Ruler, and Dorothee Sölle, who generally see Christ as only the

---

[10]Braaten, "A Trinitarian Theology of the Cross," 114-15, criticizes Moltmann for this neglect and especially notes his failure to treat the concept of substitution.

anticipation of the end, as God's lieutenant, or as God's provisional representative (*CG* 257-63, *FOH* 24-29). Moltmann argues that Christ is truly the mediator who creates new possibilities for mankind. He further suggests that 1 Corinthians 15:24-28 depicts a "process within the Trinity" based on Christ's eternal sonship rather than an eschatological subordination of one member of the Trinity (*CG* 264-66).

THE CRUCIFIED GOD
AND MOLTMANN'S THEODICY

As Moltmann's thought has increasingly focused on the crucifixion of Christ and the theodicy issue, he has begun more frequently to affirm the passion of God and divine suffering. Critics have been quick to call this later phase of his theology patripassianist and theopaschite.[11] Although Moltmann feels he has avoided these ancient heresies in their crudest forms, he acknowledges that his understanding of God, based on his Christology, is nontraditional. Most mainstream Christian theologians, at least until the nineteenth century, readily affirmed the impassibility of God. That God was without "passions" was a foregone conclusion of orthodox Christian theism.[12] By his affirmation of divine suffering, however, Moltmann has joined a growing wave of theologians and philosophers who have either criticized the doctrine of impassibility or openly argued for the suffering of God.[13]

---

[11]For example, Richard Bauckham, "Moltmann's Eschatology of the Cross," *Scottish Journal of Theology* 30 (1977): 308, calls Moltmann's theology "boldly theopaschite."

[12]For example, see the Westminster Confession of Faith or the Thirty-nine Articles of Religion, John H. Leith, *Creeds of the Churches*, rev. ed. (Richmond: John Knox Press, 1973) 197, 266.

[13]In *CG* Moltmann cites Kazoh Kitamori, Karl Rahner, Hans Urs von Balthasar, H. Mühlen, Hans Küng, Eberhard Jüngel, H.-G. Geyer, and Karl Barth as being critical of divine impassibility. For a recent treatment of this type of literature, see S. Paul Schilling, *God and Human Anguish* (Nashville: Abingdon Press, 1977) 235-60. Moltmann reviews some of the

Moltmann's theodicy involves the double claim that the passion of God (1) avoids the problems of atheism or theism and also
(2) provides a solid foundation for a Christian theodicy. Human
suffering is alleviated by the recognition that God suffers with us
in the present and that eschatologically our suffering will be transformed into a final joy. Here Moltmann is balancing the eschatological emphasis that brought him to international attention with
his later emphasis on the active participation of God in the present
human predicament. Perhaps the best way to enter into Moltmann's argument is to begin with his critique of the alternative
theodicies—atheism and theism—and then return to his constructive proposal.

Moltmann's critique of traditional theism is based partially on
Luther's contrast between the natural theology of medieval Scholasticism and the biblically based "theology of the cross." He especially criticizes the *analogia entis* and the attempt to infer the
nature and attributes of God from the natural world. The God of
this theistic line of thought is immutable and impassible, and the
doctrine of the Trinity is not central to understanding God. Moltmann's response, already noted, is that a Christian view of God
must begin with the cross of Christ as a divine event. Consequently, the Christian faith is not a "radical monotheism" (CG 215).
"God cannot suffer, God cannot die says theism, in order to bring
suffering, mortal being under his protection. God suffered in the
suffering of Jesus, God died on the cross of Christ, says Christian
faith, so that we might live and rise again in his future" (CG 216).
Despite this sharp critique of theism, Moltmann acknowledges that
in a one-sided way it made a valuable contribution. To describe God
as immutable guarantees that God does not change like creatures,
yet theism was wrong to go to the extreme of denying any muta-

---

literature on divine suffering in *The Trinity and the Kingdom: The Doctrine
of God,* trans. Margaret Kohl (San Francisco: Harper & Row, 1981) 21-60.
Moltmann has not developed his basic perspective on divine suffering
since *The Crucified God,* but the idea appears in works such as *Experiences
of God,* trans. Margaret Kohl (Philadelphia: Fortress Press, 1980) 50-54; *The
Power of the Powerless,* trans. Margaret Kohl (San Francisco: Harper and
Row, 1983) 10, 26-27, 117, 147; and *The Future of Creation: Collected Essays,*
trans. Margaret Kohl (Philadelphia: Fortress Press, 1979) 59-79.

bility to God. God certainly is free to change himself or to allow others to change him. Similarly, God does not suffer like creatures who endure physical pain and unavoidable grief, but God might voluntarily open himself to the possibility of being affected by his creatures (CG 229-30).[14]

A major cause of the development of the theistic view of God was the "axiom of *apatheia*" prominent in Greek philosophy (CG 228-29). "In the physical sense *apatheia* means unchangeableness; in the psychological sense, insensitivity; and in the ethical sense, freedom" (CG 267). The religious motive behind the affirmation of the *apatheia* of God was a concern to guarantee the self-sufficiency and perfection of God. Divine *apatheia* insured that God was not deficient in any way and could not be the cause of any evil. The ideal for human life was to achieve *apatheia* and avoid all passions or *pathos*. The adoption of this principle had disastrous consequences for Christian theology, for it is incompatible with the biblical perception of God's love, wrath, and empathy for the human situation. Divine *apatheia* joined immutability and impassibility as cardinal characteristics of God; hence the passion of Christ was not taken as a basic clue to God's nature. Divine *apatheia* complicated the christological development of the early church in that there was no honest recognition of the suffering Christ as divine. He suffered only "according to the flesh," or in his humanity. The two-natures Christology of Nicea and Chalcedon was an unsuccessful attempt to overcome the problem created by the "axiom of *apatheia*" (CG 227-31). Moltmann notes an indirect influence of the *apatheia* theme on Protestant liberalism. Although liberalism developed a "Christology from below," it refused to grant Jesus' Godforsakenness on the cross. The immutability of God had been transferred to the consciousness of Jesus, and Jesus was often seen as a stoic.[15]

---

[14]Langdon Gilkey, *Reaping the Whirlwind: A Christian Interpretation of History* (New York: Seabury Press, 1976) 235, argues that Moltmann needs to develop this emphasis on the self-limitation of God in order to take more account of human freedom.

[15]Moltmann, "The 'Crucified God,' " 289-90.

If Moltmann's critique of theism represents a kind of internal apologetic, one designed to correct an inherited theological position, his critique of atheism is an external apologetic, designed to counteract a strong attack on Christianity by those outside the theological circle. According to Moltmann, atheism is similar to theism, indeed it is "the brother of theism," because they both try to argue for the existence/nonexistence of God from the presupposition of a "community of being" between finite and infinite reality (*CG* 219-21; cf. *CG* 249). Whereas theism infers an infinite God from the order and goodness of the world, atheism notes only the pain and misery of the world and concludes there is no God. Moltmann is especially impressed with the protest atheism of figures such as Dostoevsky's Ivan Karamazov and Albert Camus. Moltmann recognizes that much modern atheism takes human suffering as the basis for denial of God. He quotes Georg Büchner: "Why do I suffer? That is the rock of atheism" (*HP* 32). Their protest is well founded insofar as they are attacking the theistic view of God as an insensitive being incapable of suffering. He is also sympathetic to the negative theology of Max Horkheimer, which protests all forms of idolatry on behalf of the "wholly other." Following Ernst Bloch, Moltmann suggests these modern versions of atheism can accurately be described as "atheism for God's sake" because of their concern for the justice of God (*CG* 252).

Despite his sympathetic analysis of protest atheism, Moltmann argues it has gone too far in substituting man for God as the supreme being. "It thinks of man at God's expense as a powerful, perfect, infinite and creative being. It makes 'man the supreme being of man' (Marx) and applies all the old theistic divine predicates to man for the purpose of man's incarnation" (*CG* 251). The critique of theism has now led to an uncritical divinization of man and to an anthropotheism that fails to recognize the darker side of human nature (*CG* 251-52). Atheism has also misfired because it takes the theistic view of God to be the genuinely Christian view. If the atheist understood God as a suffering participant in human history, he would be less likely to criticize God for being a sadist, despot, or deceiver (*CG* 221).

Moltmann proposes his understanding of the passion of God as a way the Christian faith can move beyond the impasse between classical theism and protest atheism. The passion of God is grounded in the passion of Christ and will be fulfilled eschatologically. "It is in his [Christ's] passion and his suffering that the passion of God became clear to me, and it is from God's passion that I receive the power to resist death" (*PL* 22). The companionship of the suffering God encourages and supports the suffering person in the present, and then the consummation of history will produce the final joy.

> God experiences history in order to effect history. He goes out of himself in order to gather into himself. He is vulnerable, takes suffering and death on himself in order to heal, to liberate and to confer new life. The history of God's suffering in the passion of the Son and the sighings of the Spirit serves the history of God's joy in the Spirit and his completed felicity at the end (*CPS* 64).

Although the primary basis for this emphasis on the passion of God is Moltmann's concern to develop a consistent theology of the cross, several other influences have been at work in his development. In addition to several already mentioned, only a few will be cited. (1) Certainly Moltmann is sympathetic with Paul's kenotic theme in Philippians 2, but he is not willing to use the two-natures Christology often used as a framework for developing the *kenosis* idea (*CG* 205-206).[16] (2) Moltmann is also in accord with the Jewish emphasis on the *pathos* of God, especially as it was proposed by Abraham Heschel (*CG* 270-74). Focusing on the Hebrew Prophets, Heschel developed a dipolar theology, based on the covenant relation between Yahweh and Israel, which correlates the *pathos* of God and the *sympatheia* of man. Moltmann goes beyond Heschel by insisting on a Christocentric, trinitarian understanding of God that transcends the covenant-election framework of Jewish thought (*CG* 275-76). (3) Hegel's thought exercises a powerful impact on Moltmann, especially Hegel's emphasis on the incorporation of the negative dimensions of human history into God's history and the overcoming of suffering in the dialectical, reconciling activity of the

---

[16]Lucien Richard, "Kenotic Christology in a New Perspective," *Église et Théologie* 7 (1976): 14-16, places Moltmann in the context of recent kenotic theology.

Trinity (*CG* 253-54). (4) Luther's doctrine of *communicatio idiomatum* appeals to Moltmann because it tries to break through the rigidity of the two-natures Christology dominant in medieval thought. Moltmann is critical of Luther insofar as he fails to be consistently trinitarian in developing his Christology (*CG* 231-35).

When Moltmann develops his view of the passion of God, he always places it within the context of the doctrine of the Trinity. Despite the lip service given to the Trinity in Christian creeds and liturgies, most Christians have in practice espoused "no more than a weakly Christianized monotheism" (*CG* 236). Increasingly, in modern theology, the Trinity has been dismissed as irrelevant theological speculation (e.g., Schleiermacher). Moltmann, however, joins the tradition of Hegel and Barth in making the Trinity absolutely central to the Christian faith. He even criticizes Barth for not being sufficiently trinitarian in his approach, that is, for still using a "simple concept of God" (*CG* 203). In addition, Moltmann agrees with Karl Rahner's judgment that the distinction between the economic trinity and the immanent trinity is artificial and unnecessary (*CG* 239-40). In *The Trinity and the Kingdom*, Moltmann elaborates his doctrine of the Trinity, showing the relation of the Trinity to the suffering of God. In all of his discussions of the Trinity, Moltmann tries to avoid some of the excesses of trinitarian speculation by rooting this doctrine in the passion of Christ.

> If the cross of Jesus is understood as a divine event, i.e. as an event between Jesus and his God and Father, it is necessary to speak in trinitarian terms of the Son and the Father and the Spirit. In that case the doctrine of the Trinity is no longer an exorbitant and impractical speculation about God, but is nothing other than a shorter version of the passion narrative of Christt. . . . The form of the crucified Christ is the Trinity (*CG* 246).

Because God is actively involved in the death and resurrection of Jesus, Jesus' experience correlates with that of God. Despite this unity of experience, Moltmann is reluctant to speak of the "death of God" as the basis or starting point for Christian theology. He is willing to grant the value of the "death of God" as a general metaphor, but it cannot be pressed too literally. "The Son suffers and dies on the cross. The Father suffers with him, but not in the same way" (*CG* 203). Jesus' death may lead to the experience of death *in*

God, but it is not strictly the death *of* God (*CG* 207). Moltmann further argues that by this trinitarian interpretation of the cross, he has avoided the ancient heresies of patripassianism and theopaschitism. "The Son suffers dying, the Father suffers the death of the Son" (*CG* 243).[17] The same event, in other words, is experienced differently by the Son and the Father. The Son suffers the agony of Godforsakenness and the pain of the cross, but the Father suffers the grief of the death of his Son.

In several places Moltmann addresses the issue of what prompts or evokes the passion of God. God suffers preeminently because of the death of the Son. Moltmann especially likes the emphasis of John and Paul that God gave up his Son to the cross because of his love for mankind (Rom. 8:32, Gal. 2:20, John 3:16, Eph. 5:25) (*CG* 191-93, 241-49). He notes that the term "deliver up" (*paradidonai*) has a negative connotation in passages like Romans 1:18-32, where it is associated with the wrath of God, but Paul introduces a radical change when he uses it to interpret the passion of Christ. The Father's giving up of Christ becomes the basis for God's justification of the godless (Rom. 8:31-32). Moltmann is quick to add, however, that the same formula is used with Christ as the subject in Galatians 2:20, indicating a basic conformity of will between Father and Son. The Johannine emphasis that God is essentially love is crucial, then, for Moltmann's view of God.[18] He clearly identifies the ability to suffer with the ability to love. A God who is unable to suffer is a loveless God, much like Aristotle's unmoved mover (*CG* 222). God also suffers because he allows himself to be affected by the human situation. "God is unconditional love, because he takes

---

[17]Braaten, "A Trinitarian Theology of the Cross," 117-18, criticizes Moltmann for using language about the suffering of God but not giving a sustained treatment of patripassianism.

[18]Bauckham, "Moltmann's Eschatology of the Cross," 309-10, faults Moltmann for having a "near-Marcionite" view of God. "It seems that it would be less accurate to say that Moltmann's God is love than that he becomes love. . . . In the process of salvation history God not only reveals himself but actually becomes himself." As I note later in this chapter, Moltmann could avoid some of this kind of criticism by more explicitly developing his understanding of the relation of God to the world.

on himself grief at the contradiction in man and does not angrily
suppress this contradiction. God allows himself to be forced out.
God suffers, God allows himself to be crucified and is crucified, and
in this consummates his unconditional love that is so full of hope"
(*CG* 248).

Although Moltmann uses the passion of God as a major theme
in his theodicy, he has not yet worked out the full implications of
this view for the issue of suffering. As we noted earlier, he does
argue (1) that the suffering, crucified God is a source of strength in
the present and (2) that eschatologically our suffering will be transformed into a final joy.[19] Moltmann uses the argument that
"wounds are healed only by wounds," derived from the Servant
Song in Isaiah 53:4-5, to support his view that God's suffering with
us alleviates our suffering (*PL* 25). Moltmann is fond of Bonhoeffer's stress on the suffering of God as the only way God can be experienced in our time. He frequently quotes Bonhoeffer: "God lets
himself be pushed out of the world on to the cross. He is weak and
powerless in the world, and that is precisely the way, the only way,
in which he is with us and helps us. . . . Only the suffering God
can help" (*CG* 47). God participates in our suffering and takes it up
into his own life. Here Moltmann can cite (with some reservation)
Whitehead's view that God is "the fellow-sufferer who understands" (*CG* 255).[20] Moltmann clearly recognizes that the natural
response to suffering in Western society is to feel that God has
abandoned us, whereas in fact we never suffer alone because God
suffers with us (*CG* 252-53). When Moltmann tries to describe our
experience of divine suffering and companionship, he usually relies on the Johannine image of mutual abiding (e.g., 1 John 4:17) or

---

[19]Moltmann's balancing of the present and future action of God represents a shift from the extreme eschatological emphasis of *TH*. Reflecting on *TH*, John Macquarrie rightly argued: "We need presence as well
as promise" (*FOH* 123). See Bauckham, "Moltmann's Eschatology of the
Cross," 311.

[20]In "The Crucified God," *Theology Today*, 15 n. 5, Moltmann argues
that the process view of God does not really grasp the problem of suffering. As I note later, Moltmann needs to develop this critique of process
theology more carefully.

Paul's "in Christ" concept. He also calls this experience a "realistic divinization (*theosis*)" in which "men live *in God* and *from God*" (*CG* 277). He quickly insists he is not proposing a pantheism in which the negative aspects of experience are ignored, but rather a panentheistic understanding of God.

Moltmann's basic eschatological perspective is evident in his theodicy as well as other parts of his theology. The ultimate alleviation of divine and human suffering will be eschatological.[21] By participating in the suffering of God, we share in the "trinitarian process of God's history" and in the eschatological joy of God (*CG* 255). Drawing on his understanding of Hegel's philosophy, Moltmann insists that the Trinity is a dialectical event that is open to the future. The Trinity moves toward the future realization of the Kingdom of God. Expressed in an inadequate formula, God is "transcendent as Father, immanent as Son and opens up the future of history as the Spirit" (*CG* 256). Just as Moltmann tried to avoid pantheism in his interpretation of divinization, so here he hopes to avoid an eschatological pantheism in which the prior history of God's suffering is dissolved or ignored (*HP* 50). "In the completion of God's joy his [Christ's] suffering is certainly not cancelled, set aside, and forgotten; rather, it remains as fruitful, saving, renewing suffering and the basis of eternal joy in his kingdom" (*PL* 93).

Moltmann does not allow his eschatological emphasis to diminish the need for Christian action against human suffering. Indeed, since Moltmann focuses on moral rather than natural evil, he devotes considerable attention to Christian praxis. Throughout his career he has seen the dialectical relation between orthodoxy and orthopraxy and has been especially sensitive to the social and political implications of his theology. In *Theology of Hope*, where Moltmann's eschatological orientation is given its programmatic statement, he indicates that true Christian hope should not rob man of a concern for the present. Instead, the Christian is constantly disturbed by the suffering of the present moment when it is com-

---

[21]Moltmann recognizes that his position ultimately calls for an eschatological verification similar to John Hick's proposal. See *RRF* 51.

pared with the future's promise and the church is urged to be a disturbing presence in this world. "Peace with God means conflict with the world, for the goad of the promised future stabs inexorably into the flesh of every unfulfilled present" (*TH* 21). In *Religion, Revolution, and the Future* he further develops the ethical consequences of this eschatological faith and urges Christians to respond to the economic, political, and racial alienation of man (*RRF* 37-41). He is especially concerned that Christians engage in a "political hermeneutic of the gospel" that would activate Christians to struggle against oppression and injustice.

In *The Crucified God* Moltmann concludes his discussion of Christology by discussing the psychological and political liberation of man. He argues that Freud can be used to help Christians to a more critical self-understanding and to an awareness of psychological problems needing the liberating effect of the Gospel. Moltmann argues that Christians need to develop a political hermeneutics of liberation that will produce a political theology of the cross. "The political theology of the cross must liberate the state from the political service of idols and must liberate men from political alienation and loss of rights" (*CG* 327). This political theology will break the vicious circles of poverty, racial and cultural alienation, the industrial pollution of nature, and senselessness and Godforsakenness by offering socialism, democracy, peace with nature, and the meaning of life (*CG* 329-35).

In *The Church in the Power of the Spirit*, Moltmann further develops the implications of his theodicy for Christian ethics. In particular, he shows how the church's life is patterned after the three offices of Christ (*CPS* 76-108). (1) As the "community of the exodus," the church is to proclaim the Gospel, "infecting men with the germ of hope and liberation" (*CPS* 84). (2) As "the community of the cross," the church is to mirror Christ's priestly role by sharing in the suffering of God in the world and by exercising compassion for the oppressed of society. (3) As the "brotherhood of the kingdom," the church strives to free men from every servitude and to establish a "liberated zone" in the world (*CPS* 107). In general, Moltmann has been alert to the relation of eschatology and ethics and to the fact that "Christian theology will in the future become more and more a practical and political theology" (*EH* 11, cf. *FOH* 46-47).

THE PROMISE OF MOLTMANN'S THEODICY

When J. K. Mozley was concluding his historical survey (in the first quarter of this century) of Christian attitudes toward the impassibility of God, he proposed "six necessary questions" to be treated by anyone who would deal adequately with the question of God's suffering.[22] Although Moltmann's theodicy of the crucified God could be evaluated in regard to each question, the second one can serve to focus the discussion here. "What is the true doctrine of God's relationship to the world, and, especially, with reference to creation?"[23] In general, Moltmann's theodicy is a welcome response to the agony of contemporary existence. His insight into the passion of God recovers a theme that has been frequently overshadowed by emphases on God's immutability or impassibility. S. Paul Schilling is correct to call this kind of approach "the most profound of all responses to human anguish."[24] Despite his lengthy discussion of divine suffering, however, Moltmann still needs to clarify his position further in order to answer Mozley's question. So far Moltmann has not dealt adequately with the general issue of God's relationship to the world.

Moltmann is probably correct in suggesting that we are more impressed with the political or moral form of suffering than the naturalistic one (*RRF* 205). That God suffers with mankind now and will eschatologically transform that agony into eternal joy is a good alternative to the proposals of theism and atheism. To develop a full-fledged theodicy, though, Moltmann will need to devote more attention to the larger question of God and the world. Tackling this larger issue would enable us to see more clearly how Moltmann would treat "natural" evil. Certainly God would suffer with the

---

[22]J. K. Mozley, *The Impassibility of God: A Survey of Christian Thought* (London: Cambridge University Press, 1926) 177-83.

[23]Ibid., 178.

[24]Schilling, *God and Human Anguish*, 235.

victims of leukemia and tornadoes just as he does with victims of socioeconomic oppression, but it is not clear how God is related to the origination of leukemia and tornadoes. Does he allow them to occur to encourage human character formation? Is divine retribution a possible reason for suffering? Unless Moltmann responds to the traditional type of theodicy question (If God, why evil?), the goodness of God is jeopardized. God is compassionate enough to suffer with us, but why did he let the suffering situation arise at all? If Moltmann genuinely has an apologetic motivation, he will then need to address questions like these. One place for Moltmann to focus more attention would be on the power of God. If his theology entails a revolution in the concept of God, all of the traditional attributes of God would need more redefinition (*CPS* 62). Moltmann may have been reluctant to tackle some of these broader issues because of the danger of metaphysical speculation. By taking *theologia crucis* as the basis for his religious epistemology, he clearly is trying to avoid the natural-theology tradition of medieval Scholasticism. Moltmann opts for knowledge of God in the crucified Christ rather than indirectly from the world (*CG* 207-14).

Perhaps one way he could remedy the situation without unduly engaging in speculation would be to interact more systematically with Hegel and Whitehead, both of whom he frequently cites. Each developed a full-blown metaphysical system that often raised the God-world question and theodicy in a powerful way. Some explicit interaction with the process understanding of divine omnipotence, for example, would clarify Moltmann's position. It seems that Moltmann could well incorporate the persuasion model into his proposal.[25] Moltmann has further identified his own scheme as a panentheism, attempting to go beyond the impasse of the atheism-theism debate (*CG* 277). Both the Hegelian and Whiteheadian systems can be viewed similarly as panentheisms. It may be that panentheism is too vague a term to cover what Moltmann,

---

[25]M. Douglas Meeks, *Origins of the Theology of Hope* (Philadelphia: Fortress Press, 1974) does an excellent job of tracing the roots of Moltmann's theology, though he totally neglects the influence of Whitehead. It may be that Moltmann only began to use process insights after *TH*.

Hegel, and Whitehead have attempted; nonetheless, Moltmann at least feels a kindred spirit with these two. Hegel and Whitehead, along with process theologians, have argued for a nontheistic understanding of God that bears striking resemblance to Moltmann's crucified God.

Moltmann's theodicy could be strengthened further by direct examination of the doctrine of creation and providence and by developing a comprehensive theology of history. Moltmann certainly is not alone in his failure to address these issues. In 1963 Langdon Gilkey could ask: "Why has Providence in our generation been left a rootless, disembodied ghost, flitting from footnote to footnote, but rarely finding secure lodgment in sustained theological discourse?"[26] If a full treatment of creation, providence, and eschatology would be necessary to develop a Christian view of God and the world, Moltmann is lacking all of the components to present a comprehensive theodicy.

Although other criticisms might be addressed to Moltmann's understanding of God and theodicy, the lack of attention to the basic God-world issue, especially in terms of the doctrine of providence, seems to be a serious gap in his theological program. Moltmann frequently supports his eschatological panentheism with passages such as 1 Corinthians 15:28 (God will be "all in all") (*EH* 40, 66, 83-84, 120; *TH* 88, 224; *CG* 264-65, 277-78). With such a sweeping vision of God's majesty and the climax of history, Moltmann will be obligated to clarify the whole history of God in relation to human agony. A theodicy beginning "within ear shot of the dying cry of Jesus" (*CG* 201) is an ambitious project, and Moltmann's "crucified God" may be one of the most provocative understandings of God to appear in our time.

---

[26]Langdon Gilkey, "The Concept of Providence in Contemporary Theology," *Journal of Religion* 43 (July 1963): 171. This article raises the same charge against the eschatological theologians as is found in *Reaping the Whirlwind*, 226-38.

Chapter Three

James Cone:
The God of the Oppressed

Black theology became prominent as a self-conscious movement on the American scene in the later stages of the civil rights movement of the 1960s. One of the leading spokesmen for that movement is James H. Cone, an Arkansas native, educated at Garrett Theological Seminary and Northwestern University, and now a professor at Union Theological Seminary in New York.[1] Cone gained national and international attention with his *Black Theology and Black Power*, a sympathetic response to the concern of blacks to proclaim their identity and dignity. There he described black power as "the most important development in American life in this century" and defined it as the "complete emancipation of black people from white oppression by whatever means black people deem necessary" (*BTBP* 1, 6). In *A Black Theology of Liberation* Cone examines each of the traditional loci of theology in light of black ex-

---

[1]References to Cone's books will be given in the text with the following abbreviations:

BTBP   *Black Theology and Black Power* (New York: Seabury, 1969)
  BTL   *A Black Theology of Liberation* (Philadelphia: Lippincott, 1970)
   GO   *God of the Oppressed* (New York: Seabury, 1975)
   SB   *The Spirituals and the Blues* (New York: Seabury, 1972)

On some of the longer quotations I have not italicized the entire sentence even though it is italicized in the original. Cone reviews his life in *My Soul Looks Back* (Nashville: Abingdon, 1982). Since Cone's theology draws so heavily on his personal and cultural experience as a black man, this sort of autobiographical reflection is essential to understanding his perspective.

perience. In addition to the usual sources for theology (revelation, Scripture, tradition), Cone lists black experience, history, and culture as crucial. By focusing even more directly on the black sources of his theology, Cone then developed a theological analysis of *The Spirituals and the Blues.* "I am the blues and my life is a spiritual," he proclaimed (*SB* 7). In his discussion he tries to achieve a balance between the historical background and the future significance of the spirituals. He is especially critical of interpretations of the spirituals that overemphasize the eschatological dimension. Cone's major book, *God of the Oppressed*, clearly his most careful statement so far, further develops the oppression-liberation dialectic that is the dominant theme of most of his work.

In this chapter my primary concern is to examine Cone's understanding of God, especially his suffering, a topic that is developed most explicitly in *God of the Oppressed*. Before turning to this topic, however, some attention should be given to Cone's justification of this theological program as "black" theology. Cone's preservation of God as the God of the oppressed or blacks will be less than cogent unless it is seen within the context of an overall black theology. His emphasis on divine suffering as essential to God's response to the black situation is a direct consequence of his self-consciously black theology.

THE NECESSITY OF BLACK THEOLOGY

Although black theology is relatively new as a self-conscious movement, blacks have generally been committed to the Christian faith for much of their history in America and have expressed their faith through sermons, spirituals, and other literature. Only recently have blacks become theologians in the sense of holding academic posts and writing books.[2] Because of the apparent novelty

---

[2]For a brief introduction to the movement, see Cecil Wayne Cone, *The Identity Crisis in Black Theology* (Nashville: African Methodist Episcopal Church, 1975). For good introductions to the history of black religion and current concerns, see Gayraud S. Wilmore, *Black Religion and Black Radicalism* (Garden City NJ: Doubleday, 1972) and C. Eric Lincoln, *The Black*

of black theology, many of these spokesmen have tried to justify their orientation. In this section I will examine Cone's arguments for the viability and necessity of *black* theology.

The immediate context for Cone's emergence as a theologian was the black-power movement of the 1960s. He was sympathetic to their demands and to their consciousness-raising efforts. He avoided a total identification of black power and the Christian faith, but he saw a common concern. "It would seem that Black Power and Christianity have this in common: the liberation of man! If the work of Christ is that of liberating men from alien loyalties, and if racism is, as George Kelsey says, an alien faith, then there must be some correlation between Black Power and Christianity" (*BTBP* 39; cf. 48). The black predicament in American history demands theological reflection; blacks should not and cannot be silent about the relation of their situation and their faith. The purpose of theology is to address the Gospel to each new situation. "There is, then, a desperate need for a *black theology*, a theology whose sole purpose is to apply the freeing power of the gospel to black people under white oppression" (*BTBP* 31).

In nearly all his writings, Cone criticizes white Americans, especially theologians, for ignoring the blacks' situation. White theology has been too academic and too dependent on European theology to be aware of the desperate plight of blacks in America (*BTBP* 82-90). He notes that "no white theologian has ever taken the oppression of black people as a point of departure for analyzing God's activity in contemporary America" (*BTL* 31).[3] As a consequence, white theology is generally aligned with the oppressor rather than the oppressed. White theologians may argue that their

---

Experience in Religion (Garden City NJ: Doubleday, 1974). For recent developments, see Calvin E. Bruch and William R. Jones, eds., *Black Theology 2* (Lewisburg PA: Bucknell, 1978). An excellent collection of essays from this movement is Gayraud S. Wilmore and James H. Cone, eds., *Black Theology: A Documentary History, 1966-1979* (Maryknoll NY: Orbis, 1979). This volume includes a helpful annotated bibliography.

[3]See Peter C. Hodgson, *Children of Freedom: Black Liberation in Christian Perspective* (Philadelphia: Fortress Press, 1974) for a recent attempt by a white theologian to do just what Cone calls for.

understanding of the Gospel reflects its universal message, but Cone insists that it is a *white* theology and hence limited in outlook.

Cone is sensitive to the charge that black theology will be just as narrow and particularistic in orientation as he claims white theology is. He suggests two reasons why black theology is truly Christian (*BTL* 23-24). First, true theology is rooted in an oppressed community. In the Bible God always identified with the oppressed and minority groups. Second, black theology is Christian because it focuses on Christ. Black concern with the concrete, existential situation does not outweigh the recognition of Christ as the final, decisive revelation of God. Cone also defends against the charge that black theology is racist (*BTL* 25-30).[4] Black theology must consciously protest the racism of American white theology. Yet even when Cone referred more frequently to the language of black power, he noted that black hatred of whites did not entail black racism. Racism derives from an assumption of superiority. Blacks do not want to be masters with white slaves; blacks simply want to remove the master/slave mentality altogether (*BTBP* 12-17). Cone insists that God is not tolerant of oppressors. "God, because he is a God of the oppressed, takes sides with black people. He is not color blind in the black-white struggle, but has made an unqualified identification with black people" (*BTL* 26). Cone is careful at this point to clarify his understanding of "black" and "white." He recognizes that others whose skin is not dark are oppressed and insists that he uses blackness as an "ontological symbol" for the oppressed, no matter what their racial identity (*BTL* 27). "Whiteness" is an ontological symbol for the oppressors in American society (*BTL* 30, 32). Despite these clarifications, Cone so consistently uses examples from black history and experience in the racial sense that the reader often forgets the ontological reference. In addition,

---

[4]Rosemary Ruether, *Liberation Theology* (New York: Paulist Press, 1972) 129, asks: "Is black theology just a new form of racial propaganda, making Christ in the image of black exclusivism, just as the whites made Christ in the image of their exclusivism? I believe that black theology walks a razor's edge between a racist message and a message that is validly prophetic, and the character of this razor's edge must be analyzed with the greatest care to prevent the second from drifting toward the first."

the shrillness of many of Cone's statements, especially in his earlier writings, left him open to the charge of reverse racism. For example, "American white theology is a theology of the AntiChrist.
. . ." is the kind of blanket statement that appears all too often in
his earlier works (*BTL* 25).

Cone argues that the style or tone of black theology differs from
typical white academic theology. Black theology is "survival theology"; it springs from a desperate, almost life-and-death struggle
with a racist society. By white standards blacks are nonexistent.
Blacks must strive to maintain their identity in the midst of a culture that treats them as subhuman or tries to integrate them into
the dominant white society on its terms (*BTL* 38-39). Cone insists
that black theology "is a theology of survival because it seeks to interpret the theological significance of the being of a community
whose existence is threatened by the power of non-being" (*BTL* 43).
Again, blacks are interested in survival, not exploitation of whites.
"Black identity is survival, while white racism is exploitation"
(*BTBP* 19). Black theology is also "passionate language"—the language of commitment. Most American theology is too objective,
dispassionate, academic; too often this calmness has disguised a
racist orientation.

One of the clearest examples of Cone's theological orientation
is his list of sources for theology. As I have noted, in addition to
revelation, Scripture, and tradition, Cone cites black experience,
history, and culture (BTL 53-74). He does not list these sources in
order of priority, but it is clear that theology must be done in light
of all of these sources. Theology is not done in a vacuum; a theologian must consciously interact with his personal experience, history, and culture. All of these sources are evaluated by the norm
of theology, the revelation of God in Jesus. Cone is aware that some
will argue that the black perspective will distort the biblical message.[5] His response is that one's personal and social experience is
indispensable to one's understanding of the Gospel. He insists,
however, that black theology is "kerygmatic theology" because of
its concern to take the Bible seriously (*BTL* 66).

---

[5]See Wilmore, *Black Religion*, 296.

In his later work Cone focuses again on the relationship between the black perspective and the Bible (*GO* 16-38). He paraphrases Tertullian's famous question: "What has *Africa* to do with
Jerusalem, and what difference does Jesus make for African people oppressed in North America?" (*GO* 16). Black theologians must
draw on the wealth of black experience, including sermons, pray-
ers, folk tales, spirituals, and the blues. The black experience may
sensitize readers to biblical themes overlooked or consciously ignored in white interpretation.[6] For Cone, there must be a dialogue
between the Bible and black experience. He is convinced that blacks
have a better grasp of themes such as liberation from bondage than
most whites. In *God of the Oppressed* Cone delineates both the individual and corporate dimensions of the black perspective. He il-
lustrates the individual dimension by briefly sketching his
autobiography (*GO* 1-15).[7] He highlights the social context by
drawing on the insights of the sociology-of-knowledge movement. All theology is relativized by the interaction between society
and ideas. Blacks and whites alike work within some social a priori
or mental grid, but Cone is convinced that "the social a priori of
Black theology is closer to the axiological perspective of biblical
revelation" than is white theology (*GO* 45).

Cone's argument throughout his work is that black theology is
necessary and is Christian. Cone's sensitivity to the plight of the
oppressed and his emphasis on *black* theology converge throughout his thought. Cone's emphasis on divine passion for the oppressed is a classic and crucial example of the consonance of the
biblical witness and the black situation. As we will soon see, Cone
argues that God both suffers with the oppressed and is the ultimate agent of their liberation.

---

[6]For good recent examples of the difference between black and white
exegesis, see Latta R. Thomas, *Biblical Faith and the Black American* (Valley
Forge PA: Judson Press, 1976) 20-29.

[7]Edward K. Braxton, "Black Theology: Potentially Classic?" *Religious
Studies Review* 4 (April 1978): 88, suggests that Cone may have absolu-
tized his own experience so that even some other blacks cannot identify
with his perspective.

My primary concern now is to explore Cone's theodicy, focusing especially on *God of the Oppressed*. Cone has raised the issue of
black suffering throughout his career and would generally agree
with William Jones's contention that "theodicy is the controlling
category for black theology."[8] Cone has responded to Jones's critique of his theodicy by arguing that the criticism offered is based
on an external critique that overlooks the christological focus of his
thought. Here my goal will be to give a sympathetic examination
of Cone's theodicy and to offer an internal critique of that theodicy.

THE PROBLEM OF BLACK SUFFERING

The entire history of black people in America is a story of
oppression and suffering. Cone nowhere attempts a systematic
description of this history, but he frequently cites examples of black
suffering (*SB* 20-33). Although blacks are no longer literally slaves,
their oppression has continued because of the racism ingrained in
white society. In light of the rhetoric of American law about freedom and equality for all men, the experience of blacks has been
"existential absurdity" (*BTBP* 8-12). The responses of blacks to this
oppression have been diverse (*GO* 184-88). Some of the slave sec-
ulars ridiculed the black Christian faith in God. The blues did not
explicitly attack Christian belief, but rather ignored the existence
of God. Some black writers earlier in this century, such as Lang-
ston Hughes and Richard Wright, adopted Marxism as an alternative to Christianity. Some black humanists, such as William
Jones, argued that victory over oppression was in the hands of
blacks rather than God. Other blacks did not deny Christianity but
adopted political activity as the best option for blacks in the present (e.g., NAACP, CORE).

The majority of blacks, however, held firmly to their Christian
faith in spite of the reality of black suffering (*GO* 188). The traditional theodicy issue faced blacks in its bluntest form: "If God is

---

[8]William R. Jones, *Is God a White Racist? A Preamble to Black Theology*
(Garden City NJ: Anchor Press/Doubleday, 1973) xix.

omnipotent and is in control of human history, how can his goodness be reconciled with human servitude?" (*SB* 58). Although
blacks experienced the reality of suffering, Cone argues that they
were not concerned with the theoretical theodicy issue (*SB* 73). In
brief, they never really doubted the justice and goodness of God
and never saw suffering as a reason for rejecting God (*SB* 62). "Divine existence was taken for granted, because God was the point
of departure for their faith. The divine question which they addressed was whether or not God was with them in their struggle
for liberation" (*GO* 54-55). Blacks generally did not focus on the
traditional theodicy issue because they did not feel God was the
cause of their suffering. Cone notes that the spirituals were not
preoccupied with the problem of suffering as a *theological* problem
and consequently were not songs of protest against God (*SB* 71).

Cone would concur with Jürgen Moltmann's judgment that in
contemporary life the theodicy issue is political (e.g., Auschwitz)
rather than naturalistic (e.g., the 1755 Lisbon earthquake). For
Cone, the focus is on moral evil rather than natural evil.[9] The con-
frontation with slavery, oppression, and racism has so shaped the
black experience that there is relatively little interest in tornadoes,
leukemia, and accidents. Cone argues that blacks have been willing to grant some suffering as part of human existence, but the real
problem is the distribution of that suffering (*GO* 165).[10] Even if some
suffering is the human lot, the extreme suffering of blacks is the
main issue of theodicy for Cone. In addition, Cone is critical of
speculation about the origin of evil. Because natural evil is not a
central concern, Cone does not pursue why suffering occurs.

Before examining Cone's constructive proposal, we can see how
he clarifies his position by rejecting theodicies based on (1) vicarious suffering of blacks, (2) deserved punishment, (3) inscrutable

---

[9]Jürgen Moltmann, *Religion, Revolution, and the Future*, trans. M.
Douglas Meeks (New York: Charles Scribner's Sons, 1969) 205.

[10]Jones, *Is God a White Racist?* 21-22, lists the characteristics of ethnic
suffering as maldistribution, negative quality, enormity, and noncata-
strophic character.

mystery, (4) eschatological compensation, or (5) divine racism.[11] Cone is able to incorporate aspects of some of these theodicies into his own view, but he generally rejects these as inadequate total explanations of black suffering.

(1) Cone's critique of the suggestion that blacks suffer vicariously on behalf of whites is especially strong in his earlier writings. God chose blacks "not for redemptive suffering but for freedom. Black people are not elected to be Yahweh's suffering people. Rather we are elected because we are oppressed against our will and God's, and he has decided to make our liberation his own" (*BTL* 108-109). At some points Cone stresses God's participation on behalf of the oppressed so strongly that he seems to reject any concern God might have for the oppressors' redemption. "If God is not for us and against white people, then he is a murderer, and we had better kill him" (*BTL* 59-60). God cannot be indifferent to the radical difference in experience between the oppressed and the oppressor. "There is no use for a God who loves whites the *same* as blacks. . . . What we need is the divine love as expressed in Black Power which is the power of black people to destroy their oppressors, here and now, by any means at their disposal" (*BTL* 132; cf. 136, 23-26). In this context Cone is concerned to highlight the dignity of black people as asserted by the black-power movement (*BTBP* 8). At some points Cone is more careful to point out that rejecting the vicarious-suffering theodicy and affirming black power does not necessarily lead to black racism. The goal of black power is not the reversal of roles, with blacks becoming the oppressors and whites the oppressed, but the removal of the inequality itself (*BTBP* 14).

(2) Cone is equally harsh in his criticism of the notion that black suffering is primarily the result of punishment for sin. Although Cone acknowledges that all people are sinners, he sees no reasonable correlation between the degree of black suffering and black sin. Black suffering is not innocent suffering, but still that suffering is too extreme to be a fair punishment for sin. According to Cone, the most basic human sin is the "desire to be God in human relations,"

---

[11]Ibid., 99-110, lists these as the major theodicies that Cone treats.

which is more characteristic of whites than blacks (*BTL* 193; cf. *BTBP* 63). If suffering were distributed fairly, whites would apparently deserve more pain than blacks. Cone's alternative to the theodicy of suffering as punishment is to stress the human origin of black suffering. Although he tries to avoid speculation about the root of suffering, he stresses that God is not the cause. "Black Theology cannot accept any view of God that even *indirectly* places divine approval on human suffering. . . . God cannot be the God of black people and also will their suffering" (*BTL* 149; cf. *BTBP* 124).

(3) Although Cone allows for an element of mystery in his own theodicy, he refuses to appeal to divine mystery too quickly. In his first book he insisted that it "is not permissible to appeal to the ideal that God's will is inscrutable. . . ." (*BTBP* 124). Cone grants that blacks cannot produce a totally adequate theodicy that will remove all mystery, but they are not forced to the other extreme of appealing totally to God's mysterious action in history. Cone is fond of quoting James Weldon Johnson's reference to the black preacher's attempt to "unscrew the inscrutable" (*GO* 19, *SB* 40).

(4) Cone is particularly hostile toward any theodicy based on eschatological compensation, perhaps because black religion has so often been interpreted via this one theme. Certainly black theology, along with all of Christianity, has an eschatological dimension, but Cone insists that black theology is also "an earthly theology" (*BTBP* 123). Indeed, in his early writings he argues that the ideas of heaven and reward are irrelevant for black theology (*BTBP* 125). A genuinely eschatological perspective will always result in a dissatisfaction with the present order of things (*BTL* 241). Here Cone notes a general compatibility of black theology with the theology-of-hope movement, especially with Jürgen Moltmann. In *The Spirituals and the Blues* Cone is highly critical of the interpretation of the spirituals as "compensatory" in the sense that they highlighted the bliss of heaven as a counterbalance to the misery of the present (*SB* 17-19). Cone is sympathetic to those interpretations that stress the historical basis for the spirituals *as well as* the eschatological dimension (*SB* 88-92).

(5) Cone early recognized that divine racism was one possible interpretation of the black experience. "Either God is identified with the oppressed to the point that their experience becomes his or he

is a God of racism" (*BTL* 120-21). The divine-racist perspective has been argued most forcefully by William Jones, who suggests that one way to make sense of massive black suffering is to see God as a white racist. Jones calls his own position "humanocentric theism" because it reduces God's responsibility for evil by advocating the "functional ultimacy of man."[12] Jones further argues that a black theologian can refute the charge of divine racism only by pointing to a definitive exaltation-liberation event for blacks that will clearly disclose God's favor toward them.[13] Cone's response, to be developed below, is that the crucifixion-resurrection of Jesus is such an event, one that vindicates black faith in Christ (*GO* 175-77).

THE PARADOX OF BLACK LIBERATION

Cone develops his theodicy within the context of the oppression-liberation dialectic that has dominated his theology, climaxing in *God of the Oppressed*. Cone insists that this dialectic is essential to the black experience and to the biblical faith (*GO* 37-38, 60).[14] He once described Christian theology as "a rational study of the being of God in the world in light of the existential situation of an oppressed community, relating the forces of liberation to the essence of the gospel, which is Jesus Christ" (*BTL* 17). In the Exodus, in the social concern of the prophets, and in the career of Jesus, the stress on liberation is constant (*BTL* 18-20). This biblical concern for freedom correlates with the black protest against racism and oppression. Cone recognizes, however, that his theodicy may not appear rational to an outsider (*GO* 191; *SB* 59). Black theologians must grapple with an "unavoidable paradox: How do we explain our faith in God as the Liberator of the oppressed when black people have been oppressed for more than three centuries in North America?" (*GO* 188). In his earlier writings Cone even went be-

---

[12]Ibid., xxii.

[13]Ibid., 18-20.

[14]Cecil Wayne Cone, *The Identity Crisis in Black Theology* (Nashville: African Methodist Episcopal Church, 1975) 118, argues that his brother's stress on liberation is derived from the black-power movement.

yond the category of paradox and argued that black theology might seem "irrational" to the extent that it did not fit the rational categories of white theologians (*BP* 12-13).

Cone attempts to avoid a theoretical, speculative orientation in his theodicy. The black encounter with suffering has been that of victim rather than spectator (*GO* 180). For this reason blacks are reluctant to speculate about the origin of evil, a question that often preoccupied Greek philosophers and Christian theologians dependent on that tradition. Here the black experience again parallels the biblical perspective. "The Bible has little or no interest in rational explanations regarding the origins of evil. That evil exists is taken for granted. The focus is on what God has done, is doing, and will do to defeat the principalities and powers of evil" (*GO* 179). Cone notes that John Hick's distinction between two Christian approaches to evil (the Augustinian and the Irenean) is not significant. Both approaches are so concerned with the origin of evil that they ignore the political dimension of suffering and are politically conservative. Cone is likewise critical of the traditional orthodox approach to evil for its spectator viewpoint (*GO* 181-82). He cites Emil Brunner's theodicy as an example of the typical underemphasis on God's concern for opposing suffering (*GO* 182; cf. *BTL* 146-50).

God's active involvement in history is the foundation for Cone's theodicy. He is generally sympathetic to the "salvation history" approach to the Bible and accents God's liberating acts in history (*BTL* 92-96). Cone is also sympathetic to Bultmann's emphasis on the existential dimension of faith, but he criticizes him for allowing demythologizing to slight "the irreducibly historical character of revelation" (*BTL* 105). Like many other black writers, Cone sees the Exodus event as the basic paradigm for God's role in human affairs. "By delivering this people from Egyptian bondage and inaugurating the covenant on the basis of that historical event, God reveals that he is the God of the oppressed, involved in their history, liberating them from human bondage" (*BTL* 18-19). Cone describes this divine participation in history as God's "blackness." God always takes the side of the oppressed, the "black" people. Although Cone often uses "black" in the narrower physiological sense, he also refers to it as an "ontological symbol" for the oppressed (*BTL* 27-28, 32). "The blackness of God means that God has made the oppressed condition his own condition. This is the essence of the Biblical revelation" (*BTL* 121). To clarify God's role in history, Cone underlines two divine traits: love and righteousness. Cone rejects the common tendency to make love primary and define righteousness in light of it. Such a procedure leads to an overly sentimental view of God's love (*BTL* 127-28, 138). In particular, Cone calls for a recovery of the biblical emphasis on the wrath of God. "A God without wrath does not plan to do much liberating, for the two concepts belong together. A God minus wrath seems to be a God who is basically not against anybody" (*BTL* 131). Cone argues that God cannot love blacks and whites equally; rather, he is clearly on the side of the oppressed.

Blacks have always seen God operating in their history much as he did in biblical history. The spirituals frequently referred to the Exodus, the conquest, Daniel in the lions' den, and the Hebrew children in the fiery furnace (*SB* 34-35). Although the concept of freedom was not explicit in the pre-Civil War spirituals, the "divine *liberation* of the oppressed from slavery is the central theological concept in the black spirituals" (*SB* 34). Blacks were generally convinced of God's righteousness, but they were often perplexed about why he did not act decisively on their behalf with "one righteous stroke" to end slavery (*SB* 58). Here Cone sees many similarities between the lot of blacks and the experience of biblical characters such as Jeremiah, Job, and Habakkuk. These writers raised the question of God's justice and rejected the Deuteronomic success formula. They did not reach a rational solution to the problem of evil, but they each found an answer in an encounter with God (*SB* 61-62, *GO* 166-70).

The climax of God's revelation in history and his identification with the oppressed is the life, death, and resurrection of Jesus. "Christianity begins and ends with the man Jesus. . . . In short, Christ is the essence of Christianity" (*BTBP* 34). Christ, like God, was intensely concerned with the oppressed, and his whole ministry was aimed at their liberation. Indeed, "Christ in liberating the wretched of the earth also liberates those responsible for the wretchedness" (*BTBP* 42). Jesus was the "Oppressed One," the "Black Christ" who "reveal[ed] through his death and resurrection that God himself is present in all dimensions of human liberation" (*BTL* 120; cf. *GO* 133-37). Cone is sympathetic to the new quest for the historical Jesus, because he is certain that the "blackness" of Jesus will be disclosed by a serious, even critical, study of the Gospels (*BTL* 199-203).[15] Even if Christ was not literally black, his "blackness" refers to his identification with the oppressed in the first century and now. According to Cone, one of the tasks of black theology is to "dehonkify" Jesus (*BTL* 61). In general, then, Cone's description of Jesus' character is very close to his portrait of God (*SB* 47-48). Blacks have no difficulty in affirming the divinity and humanity of Jesus, but they have not engaged in trinitarian and christological speculation.

Although Cone is alert to the significance of Jesus' life and ministry for blacks, he focuses especially on the death and resurrection. All of Jesus' life involved a conquest of the demonic powers that enslave mankind, but the crucifixion-resurrection was the crucial battle. In this context Cone introduces one of his most distinctive themes, the suffering of God for mankind.[16] Although he does not develop this theme systematically, divine suffering is the logical consequence of his stress on God's involvement throughout history on behalf of the oppressed. The God of the oppressed must also be the suffering God (*SB* 68; *BTL* 84). Although Cone suggests that God suffers throughout the history of the oppressed, he takes the suffering of God in the experience of Christ as the basic model. One clue to the suffering of God is Jesus' cry of agony recorded in Mark 15:34. Cone argues that "because he was one with divinity and humanity, the pain of the cross was God suffering for and with us so that our humanity can be liberated for freedom in the divine struggle against oppression" (*GO* 139; cf. *GO* 135). Cone's line of argument here is similar to that of others who have affirmed divine suffering; that is, the suffering of Christ on the cross points to God's own suffering.

---

[15]Ibid., 108-14, argues that Cone's concern with the new quest reflects a neglect of his own heritage, where there is no concern with this issue.

[16]Another black theologian who briefly treats this theme is J. Deotis Roberts, *A Black Political Theology* (Philadelphia: Westminster, 1974) 95-116.

Cone clarifies this claim by using the Suffering Servant image from Deutero-Isaiah. The experience of Israel was redemptive because it suffered with God. When Jesus assumed the Suffering Servant model as basic to his ministry, God's suffering was again included. "During Jesus' life, God became the Suffering Servant in Israel's place, and thus took upon the divine-self human pain" (*GO* 174). God is not merely sympathetic to the plight of the suffering, says Cone; he is totally identified with them. "God in Christ became the Suffering Servant and thus took the humiliation and suffering of the oppressed into his own history. This divine event that happened on the cross liberated the oppressed to fight against suffering while not being determined by it" (*GO* 175). The resurrection of Jesus by God is then a clear sign of the defeat of the forces of evil.

The paradoxical nature of Cone's theodicy, and perhaps of any Christian theodicy, derives from his claim that despite the defeat of suffering in Jesus, suffering still exists. The decisive victory was won in the crucifixion-resurrection of Jesus, but the war goes on. Here Cone is very close to the approach of Oscar Cullmann as he tries to maintain the tension between the "now" and the "not yet" of the Christian faith (*BTBP* 40, 66).[17] Cullmann's classic example of the tension between D-Day and V-Day in World War II is informative here. Jesus' crucifixion-resurrection, like D-Day in World War II, was the turning point in human history, even though the final victory awaits the return of Christ, just as V-Day depended on the return of our troops (*GO* 177). In principle, all the enslaving, demonic forces of evil have been overcome, but the mopping-up operations will continue until the Parousia (*BTBP* 67-68). Cone suggests that the church ought to actively announce the victory over suffering in Christ (*kerygma*), join in the work of liberation (*diakonia*), and be a place where the freedom from oppression is already realized (*koinonia*) (*BTBP* 66-71; *BTL* 230-32). "The oppressed are called to fight against suffering by being God's suffering servants in the world. This vocation is not passive endurance of in-

---

[17]Oscar Cullman, *Christ and Time*, rev. ed., trans. Floyd V. Filson (Philadelphia: Westminster, 1964) 84.

justice but, rather, a political and social praxis of liberation in the world, relieving the suffering of the little ones and proclaiming that God has freed them to struggle for the fulfillment of humanity" (*GO* 177). Although Cone earlier rejected the vicarious-suffering model for theodicy because of its stress on unwilling suffering by blacks for whites, now he can use the Suffering Servant image for blacks because they are imitating God's own role in human history.

CONE'S THEODICY: A CRITICAL RESPONSE

Although Cone's theodicy is heavily influenced by his black heritage, in many ways his major emphases are central to the Christian faith: God's involvement in history, the centrality of the cross and resurrection, and the final eschatological resolution of suffering. My concern here is to suggest two possible criticisms of Cone's theodicy: (1) the paradoxical nature of the crucifixion-resurrection as a liberation event for blacks and (2) the failure to specify the origin of evil. My conclusion is that the first criticism is misplaced but that the second criticism reflects a serious gap in Cone's program.

(1) Cone's theodicy, especially his claim about the paradoxical status of the crucifixion-resurrection of Jesus, has been sharply criticized by William Jones. According to Jones, Cone has failed to refute the charge of divine racism because he has not identified a definitive liberation-exaltation event for blacks. The options for Cone, says Jones, are to show that God is either (1) against or indifferent to black liberation or (2) definitely for black liberation.[18] Cone insists that black theology "refuses to accept a God who is not identified with the goals of the black community. If God is not for us and against white people, then he is a murderer, and we had better kill him" (*BTL* 59-60). Cone feels he avoided divine racism by noting that liberation from oppression is intrinsic to God's nature (*BTL* 121), but Jones contends that some liberation event for blacks must be specified. The Exodus, for example, may relieve God

---

[18]Jones, *Is God a White Racist?* 72-73.

of the charge of anti-Semitism, but there has been no Exodus-type event for blacks.[19]

Cone then appeals to the crucifixion-resurrection of Jesus as a universal liberation event. "The resurrection-event means that God's liberating work is not only for the house of Israel but for all who are enslaved by principalities and powers" (*BTL* 121). Cone insists that despite the lack of a liberation event specifically for blacks, there has been a decisive victory over all oppression in Jesus' experience. Whether or not this event counts as a liberation event for blacks will ultimately depend on one's willingness to let specific historical events have a universal validity. Jones feels blacks need at least one dramatic liberation experience to refute divine racism. Cone feels that insofar as Christ was identified with the oppressed of his time and was the incarnation of a God of the oppressed, his experience has a universal efficacy. Peter Hodgson is quite right to note that what Jones requires of black theology "is something that neither it nor any theology can provide with integrity: namely, a *Deus ex machina*, a miracle-working God, who will set blacks free all at once, in one 'mighty act' such as the Exodus of the Israelites from Egypt."[20] If Jones is unwilling to see Christ's resurrection as having any bearing on black experience, then he quite likely has little sympathy with any christological claim. Cone notes that all he asks of Jones is fairness in presentation, not necessarily the acceptance of the Christian faith (*GO* 268). Cone realizes his position is paradoxical, but he feels it is more adequate to the biblical witness and black experience than a simple denial of God's concern for blacks. Cone attempts to hold in a dialectical tension the "already" of God's liberation in Jesus' death and resurrection and the eschatological "not yet" of final release from suffering.

(2) Even if one is sympathetic to the paradoxical nature of Cone's theodicy, his position deserves criticism from another angle. Cone consistently claims that a Christian theodicy need not speculate

---

[19]Ibid., 116-17.

[20]Peter C. Hodgson, *New Birth of Freedom* (Philadelphia: Fortress Press, 1976) 297-98.

about the origin of suffering. "The weight of the Biblical view of suffering is not on the *origin* of evil but on what God in Christ has done about evil" (*GO* 174). Certainly this emphasis is generally correct, but anyone trying to articulate a Christian apologetic in the twentieth century needs to say more than that, especially when Cone elsewhere denies any divine approval for human suffering (*BTL* 149). "Strictly speaking, the real mystery of mysteries in Cone's system is the *origin* of black suffering. For if God is for blacks, if their suffering is neither vicarious nor merits punishment, whence their suffering in the first place?"[21] Cone correctly wants to avoid undue speculation, but he needs to develop more systematically the consequences of his understanding of God's relationship to the world. There may be some consolation in knowing that God is suffering with blacks in the present, encouraging their struggle against oppression. Moreover, there is satisfaction in the thought that God will eschatologically eliminate all pain. Any thoughtful Christian, however, will still inquire about the source of that suffering. As a minimum statement, Cone needs to suggest whether God is permitting this suffering for some reason other than vicarious suffering or whether suffering is strictly human in origin. Cone could easily attribute most suffering to the misuse of human free will and thus keep direct responsibility away from God.

Once again, the question arises as to why Cone has more difficulty explaining natural evil than moral evil. At this point Cone's theodicy is especially lacking, because he has focused attention almost exclusively on moral evil. Even if all of the oppression that Cone describes as afflicting blacks were to disappear via one of Jones's liberation events, presumably blacks would still experience disease, tornadoes, earthquakes, and so on. So far Cone's theodicy has not adequately dealt with the natural-evil issue. Cone's primary concern apparently is confessional or pastoral more than apologetic, so he has been satisfied to assure blacks that God suffers with them and supports their struggle against oppression. "Although the continued existence of black suffering offers a serious challenge to the biblical and black faith, it does not negate it.

---

[21]Jones, *Is God a White Racist?* 103.

The reason is found in Jesus Christ who is God's decisive Word of liberation in our experience that makes it possible to struggle for freedom because we know God is struggling too" (*GO* 194). If Cone wants to develop a systematic theodicy, he will need in the future to address the question of the origin of evil more carefully.

Chapter Four

Geddes MacGregor:
God as Kenotic Being

The concept of *kenosis* (self-emptying, self-limitation) has been attractive to many theologians, especially in the last two centuries. The primary text for kenosis is Paul's christological hymn in Philippians 2:5-11.

> Have this mind among yourselves, which is yours in Christ Jesus, who, though he was in the form of God, did not count equality with God a thing to be grasped, but emptied himself, taking the form of a servant, being born in the likeness of man. And being found in human form he humbled himself and became obedient unto death, even death on a cross. Therefore God has highly exalted him and bestowed on him the name which is above every name, that at the name of Jesus every knee should bow, in heaven and on earth and under the earth, and every tongue confess that Jesus Christ is Lord, to the glory of God the Father.

In recent years Geddes MacGregor, an American philosopher of religion, has developed a kenotic understanding of God and applied it to the problem of human suffering. Although he sketched out his position in several earlier works, his definitive statement is *He Who Lets Us Be: A Theology of Love.*[1] MacGregor claims, on one

---

[1]Geddes MacGregor, *He Who Lets Us Be: A Theology of Love* (New York: Seabury Press, 1975). Because all the major themes of MacGregor's kenoticism appear in this volume, references will be given in the text by page number. For further background, see Geddes MacGregor, *Introduction to Religious Philosophy* (Boston: Houghton Mifflin Co., 1959) 252-88, and *Philosophical Issues in Religious Thought* (Boston: Houghton Mifflin Co., 1973) 147-73.

hand, that his view does not entail any radical change in traditional doctrine or liturgy. He recognizes that many others have used the kenosis theme prominently in their thought. On the other hand, however, he grants that by orthodox standards he is technically a heretic due to his affirmation of divine suffering. He even admits to being a patripassianist (4, 21). MacGregor's theology and theodicy are highly provocative and offer a viable response to human suffering that avoids many of the problems associated with classical theism. He insists that "the kenotic insight is perhaps the most profound and useful in the history of Christian thought and by far the most promising for its future" (94). MacGregor is one of several contemporary theologians who have revitalized the kenotic motif; in fact, he has pursued it more rigorously than most.[2]

THE KENOTIC TRADITION

Before turning to MacGregor's version of kenotic theology, we need to sketch briefly earlier treatments of this theme. MacGregor is well aware of previous kenotic thought, but he does not systematically review that history in any detail. He does point out the highlights in that history and tries to move beyond these earlier formulations. In addition, MacGregor never engages in an intense exegetical study of the Philippian text. My concern here, then, is to review some of the salient features of the biblical and theological tradition about kenosis.

In Philippians 2:7 Paul suggests that Christ "emptied himself (*heauton ekenosen*), taking the form of a servant (*morphe doulou*)." The term *kenosis* is derived from the Greek root *kenoo*. The Philippian passage has been hotly debated by New Testament scholars and

---

[2]Lucien Richard, "Kenotic Christology in a New Perspective," *Église et Théologie* 7 (1976): 5-39, surveys recent kenoticism but does not include MacGregor. See also John Macquarrie, *The Humility of God* (Philadelphia: Westminster Press, 1978), and W. H. Vanstone, *The Risk of Love* (New York: Oxford University Press, 1978). A fuller kenotic Christology appears in Lucien Richard, *A Kenotic Christology: In the Humanity of Jesus the Christ, the Compassion of God* (Lanham MD: University Press of America, 1982).

theologians, but one can find some consensus on several issues.[3] First, the text affirms the pre-existence of Christ by pointing to Christ's being in "the form of God." Second, the text affirms the reality of Jesus' humanity in "the form of a servant." Third, Christ was exalted (*plerosis*) to the status of Lord through his resurrection and ascension. Fourth, redemption for mankind was accomplished by Christ's kenosis. Although kenosis is most prominent in Philippians, several texts add support, including 2 Corinthians 8:9, John 3:13, 16:28, 17:5, and Romans 15:3. Despite the prominence of kenosis in the New Testament, other christological models were available.[4]

In the history of Christian thought the kenotic theme has been dealt with frequently, but it has been more attractive in the last century and a half than perhaps in any other era. In the patristic and medieval periods, the influence of Greek philosophy prompted a modification of Christology. One of the basic shifts was from a two-stage Christology (kenosis-plerosis) to a dual-nature Christology (divine and human), epitomized in the confession of Chalcedon in A. D. 451. As I noted in chapter 1, the Greek emphasis on deity as self-sufficient, immutable, eternal, and impassible gradually won a wide acceptance. In light of this development, one common interpretation of the Philippians text referred merely to the veiling or disguising of God's glory during the Incarnation but not to a genuine self-limitation.[5] The early church fathers occasionally used the kenotic motif, but the Arian controversy crystallized the discussion and resulted in a de-emphasis on kenosis. The Arians argued that Christ's being "in the form of God" referred to

---

[3]Donald G. Dawe, *The Form of a Servant: A Historical Analysis of the Kenotic Motif* (Philadelphia: Westminster Press, 1963) 50. For other brief statements of the current consensus, see Richard, "Kenotic Christology," 27-28, and Russell F. Aldwinckle, *More Than Man: A Study in Christology* (Grand Rapids: William B. Eerdmans, 1976) 183-84.

[4]For a brief introduction to christological models, see Aldwinckle, *More Than Man*, and John Knox, *The Humanity and Divinity of Christ* (Cambridge: Cambridge University Press, 1967).

[5]Dawe, *The Form of a Servant*, 30-31.

his being subordinate to the Father. The orthodox responded that the Logos was coeternal with the Father. In the Incarnation the divine and human natures were united. The Son as divine is immutable and impassible like the Father. The exaltation (plerosis) was simply Christ's return to his prior heavenly position. Only in the mystical piety of the Middle Ages did the kenosis theme appear with a vitality anywhere near its biblical form.[6] MacGregor criticizes theologians in the early and medieval periods in part for being cryptomonophysite and cryptodocetic; that is, they de-emphasized the true humanity of Christ and spoke exclusively of his deity.[7] The true kenotic Christology was virtually lost in this period.

The Protestant Reformation brought a revival of the kenotic motif and a fresh awareness of Christ's humanity. Luther, in particular, tried to revive the two-stage type of Christology, but Calvin kept closer to the Chalcedonian framework.[8] Neither broke radically with the tradition, however, and "their treatments of the exact nature of the divine emptying were sketchy and enigmatic."[9] Fuller discussions of the theme came in Lutheran and Reformed orthodoxy in the seventeenth and eighteenth centuries. Lutherans developed the *communicatio idiomatum* theme, while Reformed theologians assumed the finite cannot encompass the infinite (*finitum non capax infiniti*). MacGregor recognizes that because of this divergence between the two traditions, the Lutheran tradition has been more congenial to kenosis as a christological model. The Lutherans usually accused the Calvinists of "artificially gluing the two natures of Christ together like two boards" because of their failure to allow for any real reciprocity between the divine and the human. The kenosis theme was appropriated more directly in some

---

[6]Ibid., 64-66.

[7]Geddes MacGregor, "The Kenosis," *Anglican Theological Review* 45 (January 1963): 75.

[8]Dawe, *The Form of a Servant*, 70.

[9]Ibid., 73.

forms of evangelical piety (e.g., Zinzendorf, the Wesleys) than in orthodox dogmatics.[10]

The flourishing of kenotic Christology occurred in the nineteenth and early twentieth centuries in Germany and England. Several "mediating" theologians used the kenotic model to reconcile the findings of historical criticism of the Bible and traditional orthodox formulations. In Germany the main representatives of this movement were I. A. Dorner, Gottfried Thomasius, W. F. Gess, August Ebrard, Bishop Martensen, and Ernst Neander. In England the movement included Charles Gore, A. M. Fairbairn, P. T. Forsyth, Frank Weston, E. H. Gifford, and H. R. Mackintosh. Some of the proposals were innovative, even if they did not win total acceptance. Thomasius, for example, distinguished between two types of divine attributes. The immanent attributes refer to the interrelatedness of the three members of the Trinity; these attributes included God's moral characteristics (truth, love, holiness, etc.). The relational attributes were omnipotence, omniscience, and omnipresence, and concerned God's relation to the world. In the kenosis Christ laid aside the relational attributes, but retained the immanent attributes. By this distinction, Thomasius could account for the humanity and limitations of Jesus.

A more radical version of kenoticism appeared in Hegel's philosophy and among the left-wing Hegelians. Rather than trying to fit kenosis within the traditional christological framework, these figures took kenosis as the key to all of reality and to God's nature.[11] The left-wing Hegelians failed, however, to retain Hegel's dialectical understanding of reality and tended to move toward pantheism (e.g., David F. Strauss) or atheism (e.g., Karl Marx).[12]

---

[10]Ibid., 83-85.

[11]Ibid., 104-26.

[12]See, for example, David Friedrich Strauss, *The Life of Jesus Critically Examined*, trans. George Eliot, ed. Peter C. Hodgson (Philadelphia: Fortress Press, 1972). Hodgson notes the development of Strauss's pantheism out of Hegel's dialectic and its similarity with the thought of Altizer (xv, xviii). See Thomas J. J. Altizer, *The Gospel of Christian Atheism* (Philadelphia: Westminster Press, 1966) esp. 62-69.

Since the Middle Ages Roman Catholic theologians have not been sympathetic to the kenotic motif.[13] The devotion to the Sacred Heart that flourished in the eighteenth century and the theology of John Henry Newman represent the major exceptions. In the twentieth century kenosis has been discussed favorably by Hans Küng, Karl Rahner, and Urs von Balthasar.[14]

Kenosis has been a pervasive theme in Eastern Orthodox thought throughout its history.[15] Theologians such as S. N. Bulgakov stressed the kenotic theme, but kenosis is a fundamental dimension of the Russian mentality. George Fedotov noted the prominence of "Russian kenoticism" in lay piety in the tenth through the thirteenth centuries.[16] In a similar way Gorodetzky analyzed the kenotic mood of nineteenth-century Russian Christianity.[17]

In the first half of the twentieth century, kenosis received serious consideration from Emil Brunner and Karl Barth, partly because of the influence of Kierkegaard. Writing in 1963, Dawe notes that Barth's analysis of kenosis is "the most extensive on the contemporary scene."[18] One of Barth's major contributions to the discussion is his reversal of the usual approach to kenoticism.[19] Most have argued in an a priori fashion: given our knowledge of God's nature, how is divine kenosis possible? Barth takes an a posteriori approach and derives much of his view of God from divine kenosis.[20] MacGregor's approach to kenoticism will be very similar in

---

[13]Dawe, *The Form of a Servant*, 144-49.

[14]Richard, "Kenotic Christology," 17-26.

[15]Dawe, *The Form of a Servant*, 149-55.

[16]George P. Fedotov, *The Russian Religious Mind* (New York: Harper & Row, 1960) 94-131.

[17]Nadejda Gorodetzky, *The Humiliated Christ in Modern Thought* (London: S. P. C. K., 1938).

[18]Dawe, *The Form of a Servant*, 164.

[19]Ibid., 173.

[20]Ibid., 182-83. For an interesting discussion of "God's passion" in Barth's theology, see Eberhard Jüngel, *The Doctrine of the Trinity: God's Being is in Becoming* (Grand Rapids: William B. Eerdmans, 1976) 83-89.

orientation to Barth's.[21] MacGregor's general critique of prior kenoticism is that it has not been radical enough.

Although MacGregor does not attempt a comprehensive history of kenotic thought, he reviews several kenotic Christologies and the criticisms offered by traditionalists. He concludes that the major difficulty has been a failure to be radical enough. Most kenoticism has focused almost exclusively on Christology, but MacGregor calls for an application of kenosis to the totality of God's nature and behavior. God is always self-limiting and self-humbling. Traditional trinitarian thought from the period of Nicea and Chalcedon usually stressed the sovereignty, immutability, and impassibility of God. Self-limitation was totally out of character for God, and the Incarnation was "the glorious absurdity . . . a surprise *par excellence*" (72). To the contrary, MacGregor argues that kenosis is intrinsic to God's nature. He further contends that such an understanding of God would be more faithful to the biblical vision, but he recognizes that it would entail a reconsideration of traditional divine attributes such as omnipotence, omniscience, immutability, and impassibility. One of MacGregor's main contributions to kenoticism is his application of kenosis to the problem of evil. Other kenoticists have been so preoccupied with christological and trinitarian debates that they have not worked out the relationship of kenosis to doctrines such as providence, prayer, creation, and human freedom. MacGregor has been willing to attempt this.

THE KENOSIS OF GOD

MacGregor's starting point for his kenotic theology is the simple assertion that "God is love" (1 John 4:8). Although Christians have generally accented this attribute of God, MacGregor is astounded that theologians and philosophers of religion have refused to accept John's claim as a serious theological proposal. MacGregor is willing to pursue rigorously the theological impli-

---

[21]Despite this similarity between Barth's method and MacGregor's, MacGregor rarely discusses Barth. MacGregor likewise dismisses Hegel very quickly, although Hegel's approach takes kenosis as the fundamental clue to God's nature.

cations of John's claim, even if these implications differ from traditional orthodoxy. "God is love" is a logically explorable proposition, and it should not be treated merely as an emotional outcry beyond the reach of conceptual analysis. Although most Christians recognize the prominence of love as a description of God's action in the Bible, they usually see power as being more characteristic of deity. A major concern for MacGregor is to confirm the primacy of love as *the* defining characteristic of God.

Before developing his theology further, MacGregor addresses three critical targets: the immutability tradition, the traditional doctrine of the Trinity, and the idolatry of power. (1) The classic Greek understanding of deity included immutability as a major theme. Although early Greek mythology was highly anthropomorphic, writers such as Homer and Hesiod stressed how easily the gods and goddesses accomplished their tasks and how immune they were to the effects of other forces (23-25). Underlying this mythology was a worship of power common to many primitive religions. Early in Greek history the immutability of the gods was joined with their impassibility; but this whole tradition was not finalized until the work of Parmenides, who described Being as eternal, complete, and immutable. Plato later concurred that God is unchanging and unaffected by temporal events, although Plato was then compelled to attribute creation to the demiurge. Aristotle further solidified the tradition by arguing that God, as the unmoved mover, affects the world like a divine magnet. The world is drawn to God because of its love (*eros*) for Him. "What the Greeks had groped for from Homer to Plato now receives explicit metaphysical expression: God is to the universe as is a magnet to a box of nails" (38). This immutability tradition is appropriated by Neoplatonism, especially Plotinus, and finds its way into Christian theology through Augustine. Augustine's synthesis of Christian and Neoplatonic thought was possible because of the development of the doctrine of the Trinity. Although MacGregor is critical of this immutability tradition, he is careful to stress the immutable, unchanging character of God's love. "The immutability *is* the love, the love immutability" (92). The Christian needs to affirm the dependability of God, but theologians err when they describe God as resembling too closely Aristotle's unmoved mover.

(2) The effort by Augustine and others to synthesize the immutable, impassible God of the Greeks with the living, dynamic God of the Christian faith forms the general context for the trinitarian speculation of early Christian history. MacGregor's primary question here is: Is the doctrine of the Trinity otiose? Although MacGregor is quite critical of traditional formulations of this doctrine, he insists that he is not trying to abolish the doctrine. He is concerned, however, to find a better theological model to express what the doctrine was originally designed to express (55). He argues that the emphasis on *three* persons by the early councils was partly determined by non-Christian factors (e.g., Gnosticism). The concern of the councils to stress the unity of Father and Son was commendable, but the influence of Greek metaphysics resulted in a subordination of the Son. If the Father is majestic, eternal, and immutable, and the Son is human, accessible, and present in time, then the Son appears to be less divine than the Father.

The concept to which MacGregor is most receptive in the trinitarian debates is the *perichoresis* doctrine of John of Damascus because of its emphasis on the interpenetration of the three persons of the Trinity. Above all, *perichoresis* symbolizes that "the Godhead is not static but the dynamic art of divine love" (50). MacGregor recognizes, though, that such a view implies Sabellianism, an early heresy which stated that God the Father experienced the suffering and death of the Son. Orthodoxy insisted that only the Son was incarnate and suffered; the Father was immune to that experience because of his immutability and impassibility. MacGregor is willing to give more theological weight to the biblical anthropomorphisms than classical theism (e.g., the father full of pity for his children in Psalm 103:13). "The father-symbol as used in biblical literature seems to be logically incompatible with the metaphysical assertion that God the Father cannot suffer" (51). MacGregor further insists that the understanding of God as love could not be stated forcefully enough in traditional trinitarian thought because of the model of divinity adapted from Greek thought.

(3) MacGregor is especially critical of the idolatry of power or "dynamolatry" prevalent in theism (167). The worship of power is integral to most religions, and power is certainly a very common form of anthropomorphism. A powerless God would generally be

perceived as a useless God (170). Within the Christian faith this worship of power is common, with the usual model for God being the monarchy. Because of this stress on God's love, he is generally considered a benevolent despot, and his power is thought to be inexhaustible. The danger here, says MacGregor, is that power rather than love is taken as the defining characteristic of God. Instead, from the Christian perspective the

> power of God is not to be conceived as an infinite degree of power understood as the ability to do everything (*omnipotere*) or to control everything (*pantokratein*). . . . The divine power should be conceived as, rather, the infinite power that springs from creative love. . . . God does not control his creatures; he graciously lets them be (15).

MacGregor is willing to speak of divine omnipotence, but that notion needs redefinition. "To say that God is omnipotent can only mean that nothing diminishes his love" (128).

Having criticized these three distortions of the Christian faith, MacGregor develops his kenotic theology by describing the relationship of God and the world. The two issues he especially treats are (1) creativity and (2) the relation of freedom and necessity.

(1) Creation has traditionally been understood as an expansion or extension of God. For the Christian faith, however, creation is an act of self-limitation rather than self-expansion (19). At this point MacGregor is drawing on the insights of the French philosopher Simone Weil and Eastern Orthodox theologians such as Serge Bulgakov (56-57, 104, 120-22). Although God has an infinite reserve of power, he does not use it in the creation process. MacGregor argues that an absolutely sovereign and independent God would have no conceivable way of being ambitious or self-aggrandizing. By definition, he is self-subsistent. The only way he can have other realities with which to interact is to create them by voluntary self-limitation. Such a creation process necessarily entails anguish and sadness. If ordinary human creativity usually involves self-sacrifice and travail, then divine creativity should also be painful. This divine pain is intensified because God does not "need" to create. MacGregor insists that "the more ability I have, the greater the travail needed for the creative act. If, then, I could be 'omnipotent' in

the commonly understood sense of 'being able to do anything' (or at any rate anything not contrary to my own nature), the anguish of my creative acts would be infinitely increased" (106). Because God is perfect in himself, he cannot enhance himself through self-expansion. MacGregor is convinced that this understanding of divine creativity is preferable to a metaphysical dualism (e.g., Plato, E. S. Brightman) or pantheism.

(2) MacGregor also uses his view of God as kenotic Being to resolve the apparent tension between freedom and necessity. He recognizes that most people see no difference between naturalistic determinism and theological predestination. "Does it make any difference to the determinative force that grips everything, whether it be called Nature or God?. . . Do I care who is my jailor?" (113). In either case there is no elbow room in the universe, no possibility of human freedom. Psychologically there may be some comfort for the believer in perceiving the despot as benign and intelligent, but the causal scheme is deterministic nonetheless. Faced with this traditional paradox of divine causation and human freedom, MacGregor suggests a radical alteration of the theist's position. Instead of God governing the universe primarily by causation, let freedom be "a principle of Being itself" (115-16). When fully worked out, this position can help overcome the debate between the determinists (e.g., Marxists) and the champions of freedom (e.g., existentialists).

The affirmation of God as love is again MacGregor's primary support for his modification of the freedom/necessity debate. For human freedom to be real, it is not enough for God to limit his power occasionally. According to MacGregor, God's power is controlled by his essential nature, love. Borrowing from Simone Weil again, he argues that "love without freedom is impossible. Love *is* the abdication of power. God is not He-who-is; God is He-who-abdicates" (120). In other words, human freedom is the gift of a God who lets finite realities be free through his voluntary self-limitation.[22] Still following the insights of Weil, MacGregor contends that

---

[22]John Macquarrie, *Principles of Christian Theology* (New York: Charles Scribner's Sons, 1966) uses the concept of "letting-be" throughout his study.

God allows a "blind" necessity to pervade the natural world, thereby establishing an arena for the exercise of human freedom. This "blind" necessity acts as a screen between God and human beings, shielding them from a direct encounter with God. Such a direct encounter would remove all human freedom, compelling the human being to surrender to God. God's motive for creating this type of situation is his sacrificial, kenotic love. Consequently, "God must be represented in such a way that he never at any point interferes with his creatures. Even *en archē*, in giving them the condition of their existence . . . he puts no restraint on them. He lets them be" (124). Given this understanding of the relation of human freedom and necessity, MacGregor insists that freedom and necessity are not mutually exclusive. "Necessity, then, far from being a hindrance, is the indispensable condition for the development of freedom" (125). Necessity in the natural world is part of the human situation, but God intends it as an aid to human growth.

A KENOTIC THEODICY

MacGregor recognizes the stubbornness of the problem of evil for classical theism and realizes it will provide a crucial test for his kenotic theology. His overall goal is to construct a theology that is "both metaphysically intelligible and consonant with biblical testimony" (98). As a result, he has come "to consider kenosis as the root principle of Being. To call God kenotic Being is to specify what we mean by saying 'God is love' " (107). MacGregor believes his kenotic view of God renders a more satisfactory response to the problem of evil than does classical theism. The crux of the traditional theodicy issue is the apparent conflict of God's love and power with human suffering. The three usual responses to this dilemma are (1) atheism, (2) God's love is defective, and (3) God's power is defective. MacGregor contends that a better solution is to redefine divine power on the basis of God's loving nature (15). Such a move will allow a more intelligible Christian account of human suffering.

The fact that God's power functions primarily as a letting-be is crucial to resolving the problem of evil. Because God restrains his power to provide for human freedom amidst blind necessity, some struggle and suffering is practically inevitable. For MacGregor, evil in both the so-called natural and moral forms ultimately results from the freedom given by God in the creative process. "Evil . . . exhibits the price of the risk that God assumes when, in sending his creatures forth, he refrains from restricting them" (136). The more freedom granted by God, the greater the possibilities for good and evil and the greater the risk of human suffering.

At this point MacGregor adopts some insights from Origen's view of creation and fall. Although Origen comes close to equating creation and fall, MacGregor believes Origen was simply stressing that finite creatures have been placed in a situation characterized by the possibility of growth and freedom. There is nothing intrinsically wrong with this given situation, but a fall is apparently inevitable. Ultimately God is responsible, then, for both moral and natural evil because he created the kind of world in which, for example, wars and tornadoes can occur. God is still preeminently love, says MacGregor, because this kind of world allows for the possibility of mature, responsible development by all creatures.

MacGregor further clarifies his theodicy by outlining three basic principles. (1) God's love is not jealous. A jealous love would result in restrictions on any rivals, but God has no rivals. "He alone can love his creatures and let them be" (141). The only limitation imposed by God on his creatures is their essential creatureliness. (2) The *imago dei* characterizes all creatures. The nature of this divine image is not specified by MacGregor, but it is more noticeable in human beings than in other creatures. (3) The traditional attributes of God need to be rethought in light of God's love. We have already seen how this approach would affect the understanding of omnipotence. However, MacGregor does not develop this part of the program beyond a few suggestions.

MacGregor believes these three principles are compatible with modern understandings of biological evolution. He argues that "the divine act of creation bestows on every creature an unlimited potentiality for development" (143). The evolutionary struggle is inevitable yet constructive as each creature strives for fulfillment of its potential. MacGregor is especially critical of figures such as John Stuart Mill and David Hume, who use the fact of struggle as evidence for God's limited power. These philosophers have been critical of Christianity because they hold a common misunderstanding of the God-world relationship: that God should guarantee the triumph of good over evil at every moment. According to Mac-Gregor, God grants existence and freedom, but his kenotic love refuses to intervene capriciously in human affairs. Indeed, he argues that "bare" existence "is the most priceless because it is the most basic of all possible gifts" (16). He reflects on his own horror at age five that he might never have existed. He concludes that Christians are wrong in presupposing a set of "natural rights" for human beings. Such a view leads to constant feelings of being wronged and deprived. Sheer existence is the highest good, and thankfulness for life itself is required. Everything else in life is "gravy" (157). Consequently, God should not be expected to intervene in human affairs to rule out all pain and suffering because he never intended or guaranteed a state of painless bliss.

If the origin of evil is due to the self-limitation of divine power and the freedom of all creatures, how does God respond to the fact of suffering in the world? Here MacGregor treats the relationship of providence and prayer and generally takes the side of traditional Christian practice against traditional theology. If God is omniscient and omnipotent, why pray? God knows all needs and could respond without human prompting. MacGregor insists that God is responsive to human need even though he limits his interference in the natural order. "Providence awaits prayer," he argues (153). When he develops his understanding of providence, however, MacGregor continues his emphasis on God's noninterference in the world. God always shares in the suffering of his creatures, but he does not interfere miraculously to remedy a situation.

> The model of Providence I am proposing here excludes any notion of divine intervention of such kind as would seem to make God an errand boy, either to carry out our whims for us or to actualize for us our ideals. The task and the responsibility remains ours; nor does God change anything or do anything in our stead; nevertheless . . . he, being in the 'dead-end' situation with us does show us ways of coping and sustains us in our efforts to cope (156).

Although this kenotic God will not intervene directly in our affairs, MacGregor contends that prayer is still eminently beneficial for Christians. He recognizes that prayer should not be concerned with requests for miracles. From his perspective God is never vacant from the world or inactive, yet God does not act magically to alter situations arising from the use or misuse of the freedom previously granted. Prayer serves primarily to alert the Christian to resources and strategies already available rather than to enlist God's direct, magical intervention in the situation. "If I pray well . . . I shall learn through my prayer how best to help my brother by putting my action where my mouth is" (158). The intervention of God is not necessary, argues MacGregor, because solutions to our problems are already here. To look for evidence of God in such miraculous events is to misunderstand the kenotic nature of God.

MacGregor's God may not do old-fashioned miracles to stop human suffering, but he does not desert the sufferer. Over and over MacGregor insists on the love of God for his creatures and the suffering of God with his creatures. He argues that God can suffer and admits he is guilty of the ancient heresy of patripassianism (4). Such a position was condemned in the early church because of a fear that distinctions would blur between the Father and Son. MacGregor does not argue that the Father died as the Son died, but he agrees with P. T. Forsyth that the crucifixion of Jesus reflects the nature of God himself (98).[23] If God is defined primarily as love, then divine suffering is a logical consequence of that love.

THE REACH AND LIMITS OF KENOTIC THEODICY

MacGregor's theodicy is certainly one of the most stimulating and provocative in contemporary theology. Although he makes no claim to have reached a totally satisfactory theodicy, it is clear he considers his kenotic theodicy to be more adequate than traditional theistic approaches. I shall now attempt a brief critical ap-

---

[23]Altizer, *The Gospel of Christian Atheism*, develops his kenoticism into a death-of-God position. Although MacGregor identifies himself as a patripassianist and criticizes the doctrine of the Trinity, he does not go as far as Altizer in insisting on the death of the Father in the Son.

praisal of MacGregor's theodicy by focusing on two questions central to his program: (1) Is God responsible for suffering? (2) What is God doing to alleviate suffering? Although MacGregor responds to both questions, my judgment is that he answers the first question more satisfactorily than the second.

(1) Is God responsible for suffering? After considerable attention to God's involvement in the origin of suffering, MacGregor concludes that ultimately God is responsible for creating the conditions in which evil can originate. God does not directly initiate suffering, but he creates a world marked by creaturely freedom and necessity. Both natural and moral evil are due to the misuse of this freedom. MacGregor rigorously opposes any understanding of God that inclines toward determinism or attributing direct responsibility for suffering to God.

MacGregor certainly recognizes that the crux of the theodicy issue is the relationship of divine love and power. For the Christian, the priority must be on love as the determining characteristic of God. Although his critique of the worship of "clout" by most theists tends to be overstated and overly polemical at some points, MacGregor is basically on target in his criticisms. The typical Christian overemphasis on the power of God has usually intensified the problem of suffering rather than alleviated it. If God simply possesses brute power to an infinite degree, the sufferer has no recourse but to question God's goodness. MacGregor is to be commended for revising the priority in the love-power polarity. The sufferer's question, "Why me?," may not be totally eliminated by MacGregor's kenotic proposal, but the force of the query seems to be lessened. MacGregor's response is that God's decision to create a world characterized by human freedom and blind necessity allows for the real possibility (even inevitability) of suffering caused by tornadoes, earthquakes, war, and slavery. Such a created order may produce a Gandhi as well as a Hitler. For MacGregor, any theology that eliminates this kind of creaturely freedom pushes the burden of responsibility for suffering back to God. MacGregor's vision of God as self-emptying leaves God ultimately or indirectly responsible for all suffering, but the sufferer must also place blame on secondary causes such as gravity, atmospheric conditions, and human greed.

Although MacGregor's theodicy is highly suggestive on the question of evil's origin, he frequently seems to be overreacting to the theistic tradition. His stated aim is to work out the implications of the claim "God is love" as thoroughly as possible, yet he seems very concerned to avoid any hint of the traditional view of God's power. Certainly the Christian God is more than a benevolent despot. MacGregor is also right in avoiding a sentimental view of divine love (e.g., God as a senile, rich uncle).[24] But MacGregor frequently seems to forget that the biblical view of God as "father" includes a dimension of sternness and discipline. MacGregor may be so concerned to avoid the monarchical model of divinity that his God has no clout at all. MacGregor would probably respond that my claim simply leads us back to the initial dilemma: how is God loving and powerful simultaneously? I am simply suggesting that he has let the pendulum swing too far in his critique of theism. He has let the kenotic model operate so rigidly in his theodicy that he has neglected the biblical emphasis on God using his clout for a loving purpose (e.g., Exodus).

(2) What is God doing to alleviate suffering? Just as Mac-Gregor's God is not directly responsible for the origin of suffering, so his God is not, it seems, directly involved in alleviating suffering. Again, MacGregor is quite right in highlighting divine *agape* and redefining omnipotence. Christians have too often interpreted Providence as God's miraculous intervention in the natural world. Such a manifestation of dynamolatry is clearly nonbiblical. Even after this misunderstanding is corrected, however, Mac-Gregor's own view of Providence does little to reassure the sufferer. His argument that there are no "natural" rights for creatures beyond the gift of bare existence is well taken, but he does not explain the prevalence of divine promises of well-being to the covenant community. If God does not guarantee certain rights to all of humanity, at least some Hebrews and Christians felt they had legitimate reasons for asking why suffering afflicted them. At this point MacGregor's difficulty may be that he is trying to account for all suffering with a single model—God as kenotic Being—whereas

---

[24]MacGregor, *Introduction to Religious Philosophy*, 274-77.

the biblical witness seems to point to a variety of reasons why people suffer. Surely some suffering is due to creaturely freedom and blind necessity interacting, but perhaps other suffering is due to the divine arrangement of circumstances.

MacGregor's criticism of Providence as "an occasional wand-waving from the hand of an omnipotent magician" (163) is on target, but he seems to have gone to the other extreme with his view of "a laissez-faire God."[25] Indeed, he seems dangerously close to a deistic understanding of God in some passages.[26] MacGregor is so concerned to keep God from disrupting nature and infringing on creaturely freedom that he borders on totally detaching God from the course of history. Here MacGregor seems to equivocate. On one hand he argues that God "never at any point interferes with his creatures. . . . He lets them be" (124) and later he adds that God "never exerts any pressure on his creatures" (125). On the other hand he seems to modify his position: "God may then be seen to be totally permissive. Yet . . . his permissiveness is matched by his readiness to intervene when our supplications are made by those who are in the kenotic way" (127).

God's way of responding to suffering is not to alleviate it by magical intervention. Someone suffering from leukemia should not expect God to drop the cure into the doctor's lap because of intercessory prayer. Such requests are "foolish at best and blasphemous at worst, not because they exaggerate the power of God but because they dictate methods to God. . . ." (159). Despite the lack of miracles, the sufferer is assured of God's presence with him in the midst of suffering. This emphasis on divine suffering, although considered heretical in early Christian history (patripassianism, theopaschitism), is reappearing in several contemporary writers and is rightly called "the most profound of all responses to human anguish."[27] The sufferer is assured of divine companion-

---

[25]MacGregor, *Philosophical Issues in Religious Thought*, 140.

[26]Ibid., 460.

[27]S. Paul Schilling, *God and Human Anguish* (Nashville: Abingdon Press, 1977) 235.

ship throughout his agony. MacGregor differs from other recent proponents of divine suffering by not emphasizing the christological basis of this position. He seems satisfied with interpreting this divine pain as a divine empathy with the human condition, whereas others have stressed the role of the passion of Christ in pointing to or confirming this divine suffering.[28] It would perhaps help if MacGregor clarified his Christology at this point. Is Jesus an exception to the principle of divine noninterference? Is Jesus' primary role that of revealer of divine empathy? Could we be aware of divine empathy if Jesus never existed?

Although creaturely suffering can be intelligibly explained by the existence of a self-limiting God, creaturely freedom, and blind necessity, MacGregor's scheme would be strengthened if he would clarify two additional points. (1) MacGregor should clarify his understanding of divine power in relation to human activity. Granted the self-limitation of divine power and the reality of human freedom, does God leave mankind totally alone to fulfill its potential? How does God present the kenotic ideal to mankind for its imitation? MacGregor does not develop an ethical system, but he sees the kenotic principle as "the law of life" (183) and argues that the Christian life should be marked by self-limitation rather than self-expansion. Perhaps MacGregor could adapt some insights from the process understanding of God as presenting a "lure" to his creatures. Process theologians would generally concur with Mac-Gregor's critique of God as despot, but the understanding of the persuasive, luring power of God seems richer than MacGregor's laissez-faire God. MacGregor seems especially fearful that any emphasis on divine causation will entail human passivity. Perhaps he could preserve his kenotic emphasis while allowing for more divine-human cooperation. Surely one can avoid the "God of the gaps" without moving to an entirely "laissez-faire God."

(2) MacGregor needs to develop the relationship of his theodicy to eschatology. He has developed different eschatological themes in several books, but his theodicy seems to be lacking an

---

[28]For example, Jürgen Moltmann, *The Crucified God*, trans. R. A. Wilson and John Bowden (New York: Harper & Row, 1974) 243.

eschatological aspect.[29] A traditional emphasis of Christian theodicy has been that suffering will be eschatologically resolved (e.g., Romans 8:18-25).[30] MacGregor's apparent lack of interest in this eschatological dimension raises serious questions about the rest of his theodicy. Is the future totally open? Does God end his self-limitation at the climax of history and act with "clout" to eliminate suffering? MacGregor has been willing to opt for maximum creaturely freedom and the concomitant suffering throughout human history, so he may answer affirmatively to the first question. By claiming that God has power in reserve that he is not using by his own choice, MacGregor has differentiated his position from the finite deity of metaphysical dualism (ix, 99). Thus he could answer the second question affirmatively. If God will overcome suffering in the future, MacGregor needs to specify the character of the *eschaton*. MacGregor's sympathy with the evolutionary model for history might correlate with a teleological model for theodicy, but he has not indicated this dimension of his theodicy satisfactorily so far. To use the traditional terminology, MacGregor has neglected the plerosis in his preoccupation with the kenosis.[31] So far MacGregor has sketched out his doctrines of creation and Providence in light of his kenotic theology; now he needs to develop a kenotic eschatology to complete his theology of history.

Despite these critical remarks, I find MacGregor's proposal to be highly attractive and a viable response to the problem of suffering. His emphasis on love as the primary attribute of God is certainly a welcome corrective to a rigid theism often obsessed with

---

[29]MacGregor has developed an eschatology in *Introduction to Religious Philosophy*, 180-220, and *Philosophical Issues in Religious Thought*, 289-309.

[30]John Hick, *Evil and the God of Love* (London: Macmillan & Co., 1966) 261 n. 2, classifies MacGregor's theodicy in *Introduction to Religious Philosophy* as a reconstructed teleological theodicy. I am suggesting that MacGregor has not adequately developed this perspective in his later work.

[31]See P. T. Forsyth, *The Person and Place of Jesus Christ* (London: Independent Press, 1909) 329. Forsyth is careful in his Christology to keep this balance between kenosis and plerosis.

divine power. MacGregor's theological program should do much to revive interest in kenoticism, once described as "a basic building block in the reconstruction of Christology."[32] Perhaps it can play such a role in the development of a Christian theodicy. At the very least MacGregor has demonstrated that "God is love" is a logically explorable proposition, one that is eminently useful for theological reflection.

---

[32]Dawe, *The Form of a Servant*, 11.

Chapter Five

Kazoh Kitamori:
The Pain of God

Writing a few years ago, Daniel Day Williams noted several challenges to divine impassibility. Several theologians were insisting that God does suffer as a result of his active engagement in human history. These challenges were so potent that Williams could refer to a "structural shift in the Christian mind."[1] Most of the criticism of divine impassibility has arisen from theologians who reflect the long history of Western Christendom, but some theologians with an Eastern background have added their perspectives and insights to this shift.[2] One of the most provocative analyses comes in *Theology of the Pain of God* by Kazoh Kitamori.[3] Kitamori, a Japanese Lutheran pastor and teacher, rose to international prominence primarily due to this one book. When this work appeared, "he was cheered as having produced the first genuinely indigenous Japanese theology. . . ."[4] Although Kitamori traces the roots of his the-

---

[1]Daniel Day Williams, *What Present Day Theologians Are Thinking*, 3d ed. (New York: Harper & Row, 1967) 172. Cf. also Warren McWilliams, "Divine Suffering in Contemporary Theology," *Scottish Journal of Theology* 33 (1980): 35-53, and S. Paul Schilling, *God and Human Anguish* (Nashville: Abingdon, 1977) 235-60, for short surveys of proponents of divine suffering.

[2]Cf. Jung Young Lee, *God Suffers for Us* (The Hague: Martinus Nijhoff, 1974) and Kosuke Koyama, *Waterbuffalo Theology* (Maryknoll NY: Orbis Books, 1974).

[3]Kazoh Kitamori, *Theology of the Pain of God*, trans. M. E. Bratcher (Richmond: John Knox Press, 1965); cited in the text as *TPG*.

[4]Kano Yamamoto, "Theology in Japan: Main Trends in Our Time," *Japan Christian Quarterly* 32 (January 1966): 40.

ology of divine suffering through Luther back to the Bible, he has recovered an important biblical theme that certainly adds a new dimension to the contemporary discussion of the nature of God (cf. *TPG* 59).

My concern in this chapter is to explore Kitamori's understanding of the pain of God by giving special attention to the (1) biblical basis for the concept, (2) his use of the idea as a norm for evaluating Christian theology, (3) the role of Japanese culture in illuminating divine pain, and (4) his understanding of how divine pain is related to human suffering. My emphasis will be on *Theology of the Pain of God* and several articles by Kitamori now in English. Except for some book reviews when *Theology of the Pain of God* appeared in English translation, Kitamori's thought has received little attention in the English-speaking world. For that reason much of this chapter will be expository, although I will conclude with some critical remarks.

THE PAIN OF GOD
AS THE HEART OF THE GOSPEL

When *Theology of the Pain of God* was first published in 1946 in the aftermath of World War II, many might have thought the book's theme was due primarily to the suffering and defeat of the Japanese. Kitamori insists, however, that the pain of God is a fundamental biblical theme and is the "heart of the gospel" (*TPG* 19). He wrote in his diary that he was impressed with the pain of God as early as 1935.[5] Kitamori does not base his notion of divine pain on any general empathy God might have with the human predicament (*TPG* 59). God is in pain because of the conflict within himself regarding his love and wrath. Citing Theodosius Harnack's interpretation of Luther, Kitamori argues that the pain of God is the "tertiary" (*tertium*) that unites the wrath of God and his love (*TPG* 21-22). Indeed, the "God who must sentence sinners to death fought with [the] God who wishes to love them. The fact that this

---

[5]Keiji Ogawa, *Die Aufgabe der neueren evangelischen Theologie in Japan* (Basel: Verlag Friedrich Reinhardt, 1965) 30-31, cites Kitamori's diary.

fighting is not two different gods but the same God causes his pain. Here heart is opposed to heart within God" (*TPG* 21). Kitamori also distinguishes the pain of God from divine sorrow over human sins. God's pain is not merely divine sorrow that he has been rejected by rebellious sinners. "God is angry at our sins, never hurt. God suffers pain only when he tries to *love* us, the objects of his wrath" (*TPG* 115).

Although Kitamori cites numerous biblical passages, his only extended exegetical work concerns Jeremiah 31:20 and Isaiah 63:15 (*TPG* 151-67). These verses share the Hebrew root *hamah*, which may mean "to growl or roar" or "to have compassion." These two verses are the only ones to use *hamah* in relation to God. When referring to the human condition, *hamah* clearly denotes feelings such as agony, suffering, anguish, and pain. Kitamori argues that a similar meaning must obtain when *hamah* refers to God's experience. He agrees with Luther's translation, the Japanese Literary Version, and Calvin's commentary to the effect that Jeremiah 31:20 clearly points to the pain of God. Isaiah 63:15 refers more to the love of God than to the pain of God; however, this love is not God's immediate love for man, but his loving response to sinners. Kitamori concludes that *hamah* refers to pain and love simultaneously, with Jeremiah 31:20 having the more explicit emphasis on divine pain. To capture the nuances of this Hebrew word, Kitamori proposes "love rooted in the pain of God" as the concept crucial to Jeremiah, Isaiah, and the entire Bible.

Kitamori does not examine the nature of religious symbolism at great length, but he recognizes that "pain of God" is a symbolic expression. "Where do we have the guarantee that this symbol is acceptable to God?" (*TPG* 163). Human pain and divine pain are "qualitatively different," but they share a "common ground" (*TPG* 167). Apparently Kitamori is willing to see symbols as analogies and allow for some difference between human pain and divine pain. In relation to God the category of pain must be analogical or symbolic. Kitamori recognizes that this kind of religious language, which moves from man to God, is "potentially fatal" and allows for human disobedience and illusion (*TPG* 55). There is no guarantee that such language is appropriate to God, but nevertheless Kitamori proposes an "analogy of pain (*analogia doloris*)" as the proper way to speak of God (*TPG* 56). He is especially alert to the many anthropopathic descriptions of God in the Bible. In a different context he notes that "pain of God" cannot and should not be replaced with a more scientific concept. He criticizes the appropriateness of Hegel's representation (*Vorstellung*)/concept (*Begriff*) scheme to the "pain of God." Kitamori argues that while the "pain of God" may appear to need some philosophical conceptualization, it is not a representation and cannot be made more precise in meaning. Discussion of the pain of God may seem crude to some, but the " 'crudeness' of theology is far superior to any human 're-finement' " (*TPG* 31). In general Kitamori takes the symbol "pain of God" seriously but not literally and feels quite comfortable with the anthropopathic language of the Bible.

Kitamori further explicates his understanding of God's pain by delineating three orders of divine love: love of God, pain of God, and love rooted in the pain of God. Kitamori is concerned here to demonstrate the crucial relationship between divine love and divine pain. (1) The first order is God's immediate love of those who are worthy. This kind of love is directed toward Christ and mankind before the relation is affected by sin (e.g., Hosea 11:1, 4, and the Prodigal Son before he left home). Because of sin's pervasive influence on humanity, only Christ is now the object of this kind of love. This "parental love" is "smooth, flowing, and intense" (*TPG* 118). (2) The second order is that pain God feels when he responds to human sin. This response is twofold. "First, it is God's pain in the sense that he forgives and loves those who should not be forgiven; secondly, it is his pain in the sense that he sends his only beloved Son to suffer, even unto death" (*TPG* 120). Kitamori uses an allegory to illustrate the pain of God (*TPG* 126). A traveler crossing a field is caught in a thunderstorm. There is no natural protection, but a mysterious hand covers the traveler and absorbs the lightning bolts. The traveler is a sinner, the lightning is God's wrath, and the protective hand is Jesus on the cross.[6] (3) The third

---

[6]Richard Meyer, "Toward a Japanese Theology: Kitamori's Theology of the Pain of God," *Concordia Theological Monthly* 33 (May 1962): 268, suggests that Kitamori is closest to a penal, substitutionary view of the atonement.

order is love rooted in the pain of God. God continues to love sinners, but that love is now mediated rather than immediate as in the first order. God is still the Father but also the redeemer; our relationship to the Father is that of sonship by redemption rather than a natural sonship such as Christ has. Kitamori does not mean to distinguish the orders of love artificially, yet for the sake of analysis he notes these three dimensions to God's love.

Kitamori is also careful to note the dialectical relationship of God's pain to his Christology. He proposes to include the movement "from the historical Jesus to the *pain* of God" and the movement "from the pain of God to the *historical Jesus*" (*TPC* 33). In other words, he is especially concerned to avoid basing his argument on a simple projection of Jesus' pain on the cross onto God's character, though he also wants to avoid any docetism in Christology. "The pain of God is in the infinitely deep background of the historical Jesus" (*TPG* 35). He notes that in the New Testament there is an apparent tension between the teaching of Jesus and Paul on God's attitude toward mankind. Jesus seems to stress God's love and Paul seems to stress God's pain. Kitamori's response is that the tension is *only* apparent: Jesus acted out the love of God in his death on the cross, but Paul and other early Christians proclaimed the cross and its implications more fully after the fact (*TPG* 40). God's action in and through Christ on the cross was not an emergency action. Instead, the suffering of Christ is totally consonant with the pain of God. "The pain of God is part of his essence. . . . The Bible reveals that the pain of God belongs to his *eternal being*" (*TPG* 45). Kitamori quickly points out that "essence" is really an inappropriate category. As used in classical trinitarian theology, this category often distorted rather than illuminated the Gospel. Discussion of God's "essence" usually reflects a "theology of glory" rather than the "theology of the cross" (*TPG* 47). The pain of God is ultimately important to Christianity, but Kitamori avoids using essentialist language as much as possible.

THE PAIN OF GOD AND WESTERN CHRISTIANITY

Kitamori is convinced that much of Christianity in Western history has not appreciated the biblical emphasis on the pain of God.

Eastern culture—especially in Japan—has a special sensitivity to this theme. Before looking at Kitamori's Japanese version of the Christian faith, it may be helpful to sketch his critique of various Western responses to God's pain.[7] Kitamori recognizes that divine pain has not been part of mainstream Christian theology. Indeed, he is surprised and worried that the "pain of God" has become fashionable instead of remaining "outside the gate" since his theology appeared (*TPG* 9).

Kitamori consistently criticizes Western Christianity's overdependence on Greek metaphysics. In Greek philosophy God was usually understood as perfect, immutable, self-sufficient, and impassible.[8] Here Kitamori is presumably reflecting primarily on the Aristotelian tradition with its emphasis on God as the unmoved mover. He agrees with many other contemporary proponents of divine possibility that this Greek tradition had disastrous consequences for trinitarian and christological reflection in the early history of Christianity. If God is impassible, then Christ's suffering on the cross cannot affect God. Kitamori argues that pain is experienced by both Father and Son because of their essential unity. On the surface, Kitamori's emphasis on divine suffering seems close to patripassianism, but he denies that he is guilty of this heresy (*TPG* 115). Kitamori also criticizes early Christian theology for its preoccupation with the Incarnation and *homoousios*, and for its neglect of the cross.[9] In some passages of the Old Testament, God and pain are clearly interconnected (e.g., Genesis 6:6, Isaiah 63:9). The New Testament also frequently links Christ's lordship with his suffering.[10] This paradoxical relationship of divinity and pain was

---

[7]Carl Michalson, *Japanese Contributions to Christian Theology* (Philadelphia: Westminster, 1960) 80, notes that Kitamori's *Theology Today* is devoted to criticizing different theologies.

[8]Kazoh Kitamori, "The Problem of Pain in Christology," in *Christ and the Younger Churches*, ed. Georg F. Vicedom (London: S. P. C. K., 1972) 85, and "Is 'Japanese Theology' Possible?" *Northeast Asia Journal of Theology* no. 3 (September 1969): 85.

[9]Kitamori, "Is 'Japanese Theology' Possible?" 85.

[10]Kitamori, "The Problem of Pain in Christology," 84-85.

not preserved when early Christianity was influenced by Greek metaphysics.

In relation to recent theological history, Kitamori uses the pain-of-God motif to criticize two dominant movements: liberalism and Barthianism. He accuses liberals of recognizing only the immediate love of God, or the first order of love; in short, they hold to a "monisticism of love" (TPG 16).[11] Liberals speak frequently of God's love, but they neglect the centrality of the cross and the pain of God. He accuses liberals of proposing a "soprano" theology. "They did not have the ears to hear the bass which is the pain of God sounding out of the depths. The 'love of God' for them was the *im-mediate* love without the *mediator*, the pain of God" (TPG 24, cf. 38). Kitamori concludes that church history "knows no such instance in which the pain of God was denied on such a large scale as in liberal theology" (TPG 24).

Kitamori is equally critical of the theology of the word of God. Barth was so concerned to correct liberalism that he made the radical difference between God and man his theological axiom. Kitamori insists that this principle is the law and not the gospel; it stresses judgment to the neglect of reconciliation (TPG 22-23).[12] Although Kitamori is appreciative of many of Barth's conclusions, he feels that Barth has neglected a basic biblical emphasis. Barth stresses discontinuity and division so much that he cannot conceive God as "all-embracing" (TPG 23).

Despite these criticisms of Western theology, Kitamori acknowledges that a few philosophers have anticipated or approximated the pain-of-God motif. Two examples must suffice. Neither of these philosophers totally grasped the pain of God, because that knowledge comes only through revelation. In his later thought Schelling discussed the idea of "nature in God" and introduced the notion of a polarity within God. God has a will to love and a will

---

[11]Kazoh Kitamori, "The Theology of the Pain of God," *Japan Christian Quarterly* 19 (Autumn 1953): 16.

[12]Ibid., 22-23.

to anger that results in an "agonizing God" (*TPG* 25-26).[13] Similarly, Hegel argues that God must embrace our reality as he rules the world. Hegel fails, however, to see that God suffers pain as he embraces the world. Hegel's "cunning of reason" is never disturbed (*TPG* 27-28).[14] From Kitamori's vantage point, neither Schelling nor Hegel really comprehended the pain of God adequately.

The Western theologian who has influenced Kitamori most heavily is Luther. He became acquainted with Luther's thought by reading a thesis on Luther by Shigehiko Sato, then a professor at Lutheran Theological Seminary in Tokyo. Kitamori consistently cites Luther more than any other nonbiblical author.[15] To a great extent Kitamori's theology is a revival of Luther's "theology of the cross." One result of this Lutheran impact is that Kitamori's theology is heavily geared to soteriology.[16] Another key example of Luther's influence, however, is the "hidden God" (*Deus absconditus*) concept, which Luther based on Isaiah 45:15. According to Luther, God hid or disguised himself and so was perceived as wrathful by mankind, although his ultimate purpose was gracious. Kitamori does criticize Luther for suggesting that the wrath of God is only the "means" of revealing God's love. Luther was aware of the pain of God, but did not adequately relate it to the hidden God. Kitamori apparently wants the tension between God's wrath and his love to be more severe than even Luther will grant. For Kitamori the wrath of God is a secondary work (*opus alienum*) and the love of God is his primary work (*opus proprium*) (*TPG* 111-12). God is revealed to sinners only as the God in pain, the crucified God.

---

[13]Kenneth Cauthen, *Science, Secularization, and God* (Nashville: Abingdon, 1969) 159-61, sketches out what the suffering of God meant in Schelling's thought as background for his own proposal.

[14]Michalson, *Japanese Contributions*, 74-76, notes similarity between Hegelian dialectic and Kitamori's *furoshiki* theology. *Furoshiki* refers to a wrapping up or synthesizing of opposites.

[15]Meyer, "Toward a Japanese Theology," 264.

[16]Michalson, *Japanese Contributions*, 93.

Without faith man cannot fully perceive God or his ultimate purposes in the cross.

Another Lutheran concept appropriated by Kitamori is *communicatio idiomatum*, "the argument that through the unity of the divinity and humanity in Christ, God's attributes are communicated into humanity and humanity's attributes into God's. Thus the human attribute of suffering was applied to the divinity of God."[17] Kitamori criticizes Luther for resorting to objective, substantialist terminology typical of Greek metaphysics in order to express this idea, but he sees his theology of the pain of God as an extension of this concept.

THE PAIN OF GOD AND JAPANESE CULTURE

In contrast with the general failure of Western theology to acknowledge the pain of God, Japanese history and culture is in some ways particularly receptive to this theme. A theologian writing from a non-Western perspective—that is, one not dominated by Greek philosophy—may discern some aspects of the Gospel more clearly than a Western theologian (*TPG* 7-8). Kitamori recognizes also some of the dangers inherent in the appropriation of the Gospel by any culture, and these will be discussed shortly.

Kitamori suggests that Japan may have had a special role in the history of Christianity. His point of departure is Acts 17:26-27 where Paul in his sermon on Mars Hill suggests that each nation has its own limitation in space (boundaries of habitation) and time (allotted periods) (*TPG* 128-29). As each nation has its period of prominence in world history, it may contribute significantly to a fuller understanding of the Gospel. In early Christian history the Greco-Roman mentality was dominant, and the Gospel was understood in terms of the immanent Trinity, essences, and natures. Later, in the period of the Protestant Reformation, the German mind was flourishing and the Gospel was reinterpreted.[18] In neither period, however, was the pain of God perceived clearly. Japanese culture

---

[17]Kitamori, "Is 'Japanese Theology' Possible?" 86.

[18]Ibid., 83-87.

may allow for a fuller understanding of this key biblical theme than has yet been achieved in the West.

One feature of the Japanese mind that allows it a receptiveness to divine suffering is its "spirit of tragedy" (*TPG* 134). Japanese people, especially the common people, are appreciative of tragic themes in their drama. Kitamori focuses on *tsurasa* as the key category in Japanese tragedy. *Tsurasa* "is realized when one suffers and dies, or makes his beloved son suffer and die, for the sake of loving and making others live" (*TPG* 135, cf. 148). In other words, *tsurasa* refers to a deep anguish or pain. Although the pain of God is an eternal truth and could be perceived in any era, the pain of God is most readily acknowledged in an age of pain by a people sensitive to the tragic dimension of life. "The pain of God can be discerned most vividly by the Japanese mind. . . . It is a truth acceptable all over the world. But this universal truth would not have been discerned without Japan as its medium" (*TPG* 137). *Tsurasa* cannot fully encompass the pain of God, since the pain of God refers both to God's love for the unlovable and to his sacrifice of his Son; *tsurasa* refers only to the second aspect (*TPG* 138). One interpreter noted that *tsurasa* is not the word for pain used by Kitamori in referring to divine pain. God's pain is *itami*, which connotes emotional as well as physical suffering.[19]

Kitamori also sees the impact of Buddhism on Japan as a potentially positive factor in the acceptance of God's pain. He is particularly fond of Shotoku Taishi, who governed Japan in the sixth century and introduced Buddhism to the Japanese. Focusing on the Buddhist concern for alleviating human suffering, Prince Shotoku asserts, "Buddha's responding sickness arises from great mercy. . . . The sickness of the great mercy saves people by absorbing their sickness. Sickness is saved by sickness" (*TPG* 26). Such an idea is very close to "By his wounds you have been healed" (1 Peter 2:24). This Buddhist idea is inadequate, according to Kitamori, because the sickness of the great mercy is not real pain but merely sympathy or empathy. Buddhism does not allow for divine wrath. "An absolute being without wrath can have no *real* pain. . . . The pain

---

[19]Meyer, "Toward a Japanese Theology," 266.

of God is his love—this love is based on the premise of his wrath, which is absolute, inflexible reality" (*TPG* 27).[20] The Buddhist view of mercy might provide some preparation for the Christian message, but it falls short of the pain of God in the Gospel.

Despite his praise for the role Japan might play in a fuller understanding of the Gospel, Kitamori is aware of aspects of the Japanese mentality that can hinder the Japanese appropriation of the Gospel. A crucial aspect of the Japanese mind is "aesthetic contemplation" or the "non-involvement attitude."[21] The Japanese usually remain detached from religious concerns and are extremely slow to convert to new ideas. The Japanese also resist the Western tendency to think in terms of opposites and divisions. The Japanese stress continuity more than discontinuity. Here the Japanese are much more responsive to the Mahayana Buddhist concept of *yuzu muge* (fusability or communicability), wherein "lies the secret or genius of Oriental thinking."[22] The Japanese mind has a drive to unity or synthesis that resists any rigid distinctions. Kitamori concludes that it is tempting at times to see the Japanese mind as an invention of the devil to prevent acceptance of the Gospel. On the other hand, it may be "an invention by an angel in order to purify the present form of Christianity and to make it the genuine gospel."[23]

Because of his conviction that Japan can have a pivotal role in the presentation of the Gospel, especially the pain of God, Kitamori has struggled with the feasibility and appropriateness of producing a Japanese theology. Carl Michalson once described Kitamori's theology as "the most self-consciously Japanese of the current theological tendencies in Japan."[24] The question of how

---

[20]Kazoh Kitamori, "Christianity and Other Religions in Japan," *Japan Christian Quarterly* 26 (October 1960): 233-34.

[21]Kazoh Kitamori, "The Japanese Mentality and Christianity," *Japan Christian Quarterly* 26 (July 1960): 171.

[22]Kitamori, "Christianity and Other Religions in Japan," 234.

[23]Ibid., 238.

[24]Michalson, *Japanese Contributions*, 73.

Christianity can be appropriated by Japanese culture has been hotly debated by the Japanese and others. Kitamori cites Uemura and Uchimura from the Mejii era as proponents of indigenization who favored the development of "Japanese Christianity" and "Japanese Theology." They argue that just as other cultures have produced their distinctive versions of the Christian faith, so the Japanese should articulate their faith from their own cultural standpoint. Nevertheless, indigenization does not necessitate the transformation of Christianity into a Japanese religion. Others grant that some Japanese characteristics will "naturally" appear, but that no attempt should be made to encourage this development. These anti-indigenization forces (e.g., Karl Barth) are sensitive to the possible distortions of the Christian faith when it is nationalized too much. Kitamori's general response to this debate is that both sides have not adequately dealt with the content of the Gospel, especially regarding the pain of God. On one side, he grants to the anti-indigenization forces that the Gospel is universal truth which transcends any specific place and time. On the other side, he agrees with the indigenization forces that the Gospel must be mediated through a particular culture. When Christianity is proclaimed to the Japanese, the use of dialogue is necessary even though one must avoid the danger of syncretization. The flourishing of Christianity in the Greek and German cultures brought about divergent understandings of the Gospel; so too can Japanese culture enrich the understanding of the Gospel by its sensitivity to the pain of God.

THE PAIN OF GOD AND HUMAN PAIN

So far we have focused attention on Kitamori's understanding of divine suffering and have contrasted it with the Eastern and Western mentalities. Now we need to examine the relationship of God's pain to human pain. Although Kitamori treats several aspects of this relationship, he does not develop a full-scale theodicy. The general outline of his theodicy may yet be discerned from his discussion.

One way human beings suffer is in service to God. Here Kitamori builds on the command of Jesus to take up a cross and follow him, and he cites the example of Abraham in his willingness to sacrifice Isaac. By serving God with our pain, our pain is alleviated. "Our pain is actually healed when it serves the pain of God. . . . Our wounds will be healed when they serve our Lord's wounds (1 Peter 2:24)" (*TPG* 52). According to Kitamori, human pain is generally due to the wrath of God and cannot be overcome by human effort. "Man's pain, however, is the reality of the *wrath* of God against sin, and is the result of man's estrangement from God" (*TPG* 61). Human pain can serve as a witness to God's pain. If human pain does not point to God's pain, it will remain "dark, meaningless, and barren" (*TPG* 52). Kitamori recognizes that pain may be self-centered in origin; for instance, some pain is due to intense love. This pain may be the occasion for sin instead of being a testimony to God's pain. Believers recognize their pain as a symbol of divine pain, but unbelievers allow their pain to increase their estrangement from God. One task of believers is to point out to unbelievers the nature of their pain. Some unbelievers may not consciously suffer, because God's wrath is sometimes not actualized. The suffering servant passages in Deutero-Isaiah symbolize redemptive suffering, but the real fulfillment occurs in Jesus and is perpetuated in the church. "The church inherited the pain of God and became the symbol of the pain of God. Each believer becomes the 'servant of the Lord.' . . . What Israel could do only imperfectly, the church must do better" (*TPG* 67).

One of the most intriguing aspects of Kitamori's discussion is his proposal for a "mysticism of pain." Kitamori is careful to delineate his view of mysticism, being aware of the slipperiness of the term. The Christian can say *"I am dissolved in the pain of God and become one with him in pain"* (*TPG* 71). This "sound" mysticism differs from ordinary mysticism and has three characteristics. First, *"we become immediately at one with God who denies immediacy"* (*TPG* 74). All mysticism stresses the immediacy of the relation between man and the ultimate reality. Nonetheless, the mysticism of pain denies a simple identification of God and man. Sheer immediacy would entail the denial of the need for a mediator and also the pain of God. The Christian does, however, identify with the pain of God. Ultimately the basis for this mysticism is justification rather than an absorptive union. Here Kitamori is fond of passages such as Galatians 2:20 that stress both the identity of God and man yet accent the role of Christ as mediator: "I have been crucified with Christ; it is no longer I who live, but Christ who lives in me" (*TPG* 74). Second, this sound mysticism results in the enjoyment of God without any concern for personal gratification. Here again Kitamori tries to distinguish his mysticism from ordinary mysticism. Ordinary mysticism stresses the enjoyment of God such that the enjoyment may be selfishly motivated. In Kitamori's mysticism the object of enjoyment is clearly God and all self-seeking is denied. "Thus the pain of God disposes of all the sin clinging to our enjoyment and God offers himself as the object of our enjoyment" (*TPG* 77). Third, Kitamori's mysticism is ethical in nature. Kitamori recognizes that mysticism often leads to complacency, contemplation, passivity, and quietism. The mysticism of pain is moral and results in sanctification. Kitamori grants that sin still presents a problem for Christians, and he agrees with Luther's maxim, "*Semper iustus, semper peccator*" (*TPG* 78). The Christian sensitive to the pain of God is aware of his need for God's continuing forgiveness of the sin that threatens their union.

Kitamori further develops the ethical dimension of the Christian life by highlighting the Christian's attitude toward suffering. Suffering is discouraging as long as it is seen as an external threat. "As long as we try to escape it, we cannot resolve it. We can conquer it only when we seek it within ourselves and long for it" (*TPG* 80). This desire for pain sounds masochistic, but Kitamori attempts to defend himself against that charge. Some of the mysticism of suffering characteristic of the Middle Ages may have been masochistic in that the mystics practiced self-hatred or self-renunciation based on their own inner willpower. Kitamori agrees with Karl Holl that this self-generated pain is merely a "pious play" that is essentially hedonistic (*TPG* 82). Real pain comes only from an external source, which Kitamori identifies with the wrath of God. "Only something *outside* the self, which one cannot command, can really injure the self. . . . The wrath of God alone cause[s] *suffering* which can wound us. The sin of self-loving ceases only when we receive this suffering physically" (*TPG* 83). Self-hatred is still essential to the Christian life, but that is mediated by the wrath of God. Self-hatred should be the natural consequence of recognizing our sinfulness and unworthiness of divine love. The immediate love of God, when mediated by human sin, becomes the wrath of God. "Yet the pain of God is the tidings that God *still* loves the sinner who has lost all claim to be loved" (*TPG* 91). Kitamori insists that sinners are unlovable and hence God's enemies. God in his pain, however, still loves them. The ethical result for Christians is that they also should love the unlovable (*TPG* 93). Indeed, loving other people is necessary for loving God. Reflecting on Matthew 25:31-46, Kitamori suggests that a Christian can shoot one arrow at two targets simultaneously. The love of God is the larger target and love of neighbor is the smaller one. The small target is set up in front of the larger one so that a bull's-eye for one results in a bull's-eye for the other (*TPG* 99).

Human pain and God's pain are related to eschatology. Kitamori claims that much Christian speculation about the End is in error, especially the listing of the times. The only valid signs of the End are the universal proclamation of the Gospel and the diffusion of suffering (*TPG* 140-41). Kitamori especially emphasizes the tension between the "theological axiom" and the "theological reality" (*TPG* 143). The theological axiom is the claim that the End has arrived in the person of Christ. The theological reality is the incompleteness of salvation in the present. Full redemption and resolution of human suffering await the End. "The Ultimate, the End, is conceived as a present reality, while, at the same time, pointing to the future. The tension arising from the fusion of these two contradictory truths is eschatological in the deepest sense of the word" (*TPG* 144). In other words, Kitamori seems to assume that some suffering is an inherent part of human life until the End. Such a conclusion places him close to the "inaugurated eschatology" viewpoint of Oscar Cullmann and others.

TRANSFORMING *PATHOS* INTO *LOGOS*: A CRITICAL ASSESSMENT

In the *Logic of Salvation* (1953) Kitamori discussed the need to convert *pathos* into *logos*. He recognized the difficulty of upholding the integrity of *pathos* while trying to communicate this truth through the medium of *logos*.[25] This fragile conversion of *pathos*, in the sense of God's pain, into reflective theology or *logos* has been Kitamori's concern throughout his career. While a full-scale assessment of his work is beyond my ability, as a theologian interested in contemporary discussions of divine passibility, I want to give a brief critical appraisal. I will try to focus on issues discussed by Kitamori in some detail in English, recognizing that he may answer some questions in Japanese writings not accessible to me.

Two aspects of Kitamori's program have impressed me especially favorably: his attempt to develop a "Japanese" theology and his critique of divine impassibility. Kitamori's attempt to write Christian theology that reflects his Japanese heritage is commendable. He seems sufficiently aware of the values and dangers of indigenization or nationalization of Christianity to take a moderate position here. Certainly any culture needs to understand the Gospel from its own perspective and avoid adopting another culture's expression of Christianity. Japanese Christianity has been dependent on Western (especially German) theology for too long.[26] How successful Kitamori is in producing a truly Japanese theology is not clear. Certainly he draws on his culture to a great extent for his basic orientation, along with a strong reliance on Luther's theology. Ogawa suggests that many Japanese do see Kitamori's theology as a specifically Japanese view of God.[27]

Kitamori's critique of Greek philosophical influence on Christian theology is generally fair. The traditional doctrine of divine impassibility seems to be in conflict with the biblical emphasis on the living, dynamic God who responds to human suffering. This

---

[25]Kazuo Mutoh, "Kitamorian Theology," *Japan Christian Quarterly* 19 (Autumn 1953): 322-23.

[26]Cf. Seiichi Yagi, "The Dependence of Japanese Theology upon the Occident," *Japan Christian Quarterly* 30 (October 1964): 258-61. For studies of the history of theology in Japan, cf. Gerald H. Anderson, ed., *Asian Voices in Christian Theology* (Maryknoll NY: Orbis Books, 1976) 179-208, and Charles H. Germany, *Protestant Theologies in Modern Japan: A History of Dominant Theological Currents from 1920-1960* (Tokyo: IIRS Press, 1965).

[27]Ogawa, *Theologie in Japan*, 108.

kind of criticism has been voiced frequently in contemporary theology and has been elaborated in much more detail by some Western theologians.[28] This sort of critique may not be as necessary in the East because of the lack of Greek influence.[29]

Two other aspects of Kitamori's thought need further clarification. (1) His understanding of the nature of God's pain raises several interrelated issues. God's pain is primarily due to the struggle between God's love and God's wrath. Kitamori is especially wary of any liberal de-emphasis on the wrath of God. God's wrath is aimed at sinners who deserve punishment, yet his love is constant. Divine pain results from the tension between these two aspects of God's character. To a great extent Kitamori is grappling with a perennial dilemma in Christian theology. To neglect God's love would leave us with a harsh, unmerciful deity, although to neglect God's wrath would leave us with a sentimental, permissive deity. The danger in Kitamori's formulation is that God seems to have multiple personalities (angry and loving) or to be experiencing an identity crisis. "But what transforms this God of wrath into a God of love? No other than Jesus himself. . . ." (*TPG* 127). A related danger is that occasionally it seems as if God the Father epitomizes the wrath of God and God the Son epitomizes the love of God (e.g., in the allegory of the protective hand in the storm). When Kitamori discusses the first order of love, however, he describes Christ as the object of God's love. Thus God the Father does love as well as exercise wrath.

Kitamori limits God's pain to his feeling as he loves the object of his wrath. He is careful to distinguish the pain of God from God's empathy with human misery. Divine pain is God's response to human sin. God might also experience sorrow or grief over the hu-

---

[28]Cf. Jürgen Moltmann, *The Crucified God*, trans. R. A. Wilson and John Bowden (New York: Harper & Row, 1974); Geddes MacGregor, *He Who Lets Us Be* (New York: Seabury Press, 1975); and the writings of most of the process theologians.

[29]Koyama, *Waterbuffalo Theology*, 95-105, notes the difficulty a passionate God would have being accepted in Thailand because of its tranquil mentality.

man situation, but Kitamori does not develop that notion (*TPG* 59, 115). Kitamori's perspective would be more cogent and perhaps more biblical if he complemented the pain of God with an emphasis on divine sorrow or empathy.[30] Kitamori has probably focused his argument too narrowly by isolating love and wrath as the key attributes of God. An examination of all of God's feelings (e.g., joy, sorrow, etc.) would put his discussion of divine pain in a broader spectrum.

Kitamori's understanding of God's pain would be further clarified if he explored in greater depth the nature of symbolic language. He recognizes the values and problems of anthropopathic descriptions of God and seems to be comfortable with the tradition of analogy. He would probably agree with Heschel's paraphrase of Isaiah 55:8-9: "For My pathos is not your pathos, neither are your ways My ways, says the Lord. For as the heavens are higher than the earth, so are My ways higher than your ways and My pathos than your pathos."[31] Exactly what the difference between divine pain and human pain might be is not always clear. Human pain is usually based on the disturbance of a loving relationship. God's pain may be similar to that, but Kitamori does not develop the similarities adequately. His proposal for an "analogy of pain" (*analogia doloris*) is suggestive but ambiguous.[32]

(2) Although Kitamori does not develop his theodicy fully, he frequently touches on the problem of human suffering. His general perspective is that a recognition of the pain of God will overcome human pain. "When the pain of man becomes the symbol of the pain of God and unites with the pain of God, man's pain is in turn healed. What heals our wounds is the love rooted in the pain of God" (*TPG* 64). Quite frequently he cites the principle of 1 Peter 2:24, which says that our wounds are healed by the wounds of an-

---

[30]Lee, *God Suffers for Us*, develops an understanding of divine empathy.

[31]Abraham J. Heschel, *The Prophets*, vol. 2 (New York: Harper & Row; rpt., 1975) 56.

[32]Lee, *God Suffers for Us*, 91-103, develops the way of analogy more systematically than does Kitamori.

other. Kitamori's angle here is highly soteriological; moreover, he does not treat the general theodicy issue. The kind of human suffering he considers is that due to God's wrath. "The Lord wants to heal our wounds, which are caused by God's wrath. . . ." (*TPG* 22). "Man's pain is the wrath of God. The wages of sin is death (Rom. 6:23) and 'death is the wrath of God' " (*TPG* 52). Kitamori might be reviving the Deuteronomic idea that all suffering (physical, mental, etc.) is due to sin, but more likely he is thinking only in soteriological terms. His usual emphasis is that recognition of God's pain brings forgiveness and salvation.

If Kitamori's main concern is soteriological in the narrow sense of a theory of salvation, it may be foolish to look for an explicit Kitamorian theodicy. He seems to have little or no interest in issues that have long perplexed Christians: for example, natural evil, the origin of suffering, or the inequality of suffering. His neglect of natural evil and his concern for moral evil is typical of many twentieth-century discussions of evil. He might consider the question about the origin of suffering to be settled by rooting all suffering in sin or by insisting that the question is too speculative to be important.[33] Kitamori's silence on the issue of the distribution of suffering is surprising. Given that human misery may be related in some way to sin, one still wonders about the amount of suffering for some. Many groups that have experienced massive suffering have raised this kind of issue.[34] Based on the suffering of the Japanese in World War II, one might have expected Kitamori to treat the distribution issue.

Two further aspects of Kitamori's theodicy deserve fuller attention. First, he needs to clarify the relationship of eschatology to human suffering. Many theodicies use eschatology as a cop-out, but Kitamori avoids that extreme. Apparently he recognizes the ten-

---

[33]Cf. James H. Cone, *The God of the Oppressed* (New York: Seabury Press, 1975) 179-81, argues that this question is too speculative to concern sufferers.

[34]Cf. William R. Jones, *Is God a White Racist?* (Garden City NY: Anchor Press/Doubleday, 1973), and Richard L. Rubenstein, *After Auschwitz* (Indianapolis: Bobbs-Merrill, 1966).

sion between the "already" and the "not yet"—between the decisive action of God in Jesus and the eschatological fulfillment of God's purposes. Exactly what this means for Christians caught in the middle is not clear. He suggests that Christians should expect to suffer within this interim period. How much suffering a Christian should expect is vague. Second, Kitamori devotes considerable attention to the ethical dimension of his theology. Most of his concern, however, is for human suffering as a service to God. Although he is aware of the need for service to one's fellow men, he apparently would have little interest in Christian social action to alleviate human suffering. Perhaps his Lutheran background (via the two-kingdoms scheme), or the aesthetic contemplativeness of Eastern culture, or his reaction against liberalism (including the social gospel) has precluded this interest. At any rate, many others who propose a theodicy based on divine suffering have shown a stronger interest in Christian programs to alleviate human suffering.[35]

Kitamori's provocative theology deserves a careful reading by Western Christians. He forces a reconsideration of key theological issues that are frequently neglected by theologians preoccupied with secularization, phenomenological analysis, hermeneutics, and liberation theology. Despite the criticisms sketched out earlier, I am confident Kitamori's theology of God's pain is a valuable contribution to the reconsideration of the doctrine of God in the last half of the twentieth century.

[35]For example, Moltmann and Cone.

Chapter Six

Daniel Day Williams: The Vulnerable and Invulnerable God

Among contemporary theologians, the ones who have most frequently and consistently argued for divine suffering are process theologians. Process theology is a movement that appropriates and adapts some of the insights of Alfred North Whitehead and Charles Hartshorne to the interpretation of the Christian faith.[1] One of the major concerns of process theology is the relationship of God and the world. Process theologians have frequently focused on the problem of human suffering, arguing that a process theodicy is more satisfactory than any proposed by classical theists.[2] As part of their general critique of classical theism, they often note that God participates in human suffering. Whitehead's description of God

---

[1]For a good introduction to process philosophy, see Eugene H. Peters, *The Creative Advance* (St. Louis: Bethany Press, 1966). For a more technical introduction to Whitehead's thought, see William A. Christian, *An Interpretation of Whitehead's Metaphysics* (New Haven: Yale University Press, 1959). For introductions to process theology, see John B. Cobb, Jr., and David Ray Griffin, *Process Theology: An Introductory Exposition* (Philadelphia: Westminster Press, 1976); Delwin Brown, Ralph E. James, Jr., and Gene Reeves, eds., *Process Philosophy and Christian Thought* (Indianapolis: Bobbs-Merrill, 1971); Ewert Cousins, ed., *Process Theology: Basic Writings* (New York: Paulist Press, 1971); Robert B. Mellert, *What Is Process Theology?* (New York: Paulist Press, 1975).

[2]For examples of process theodicy, see John B. Cobb, Jr., *God and the World* (Philadelphia: Westminster Press, 1969) 87-102; Cobb and Griffin, *Process Theology*, 69-75; David Ray Griffin, *God, Power, and Evil: A Process Theodicy* (Philadelphia: Westminster Press, 1976).

as "the great companion—the fellow-sufferer who understands" is frequently cited by process spokesmen.[3] More recently, process theologians have insisted that God cannot be "the Unchanging and Passionless Absolute."[4] God suffers because he responds empathetically to the misery of the world. As we noted in the first chapter, process theology is one of the major factors giving rise to the current interest in divine passibility. Even those who do not share the process perspective are alerted to the issue by the process theologians.

Because the literature of process philosophy and theology is so massive, I have decided to focus on the late Daniel Day Williams as a case study on the issue of divine suffering. Williams taught for almost two decades at the Union Theological Seminary in New York and was considered by many "the senior statesman of process theology."[5] Through many articles and two major works in systematic theology, *God's Grace and Man's Hope* (1949) and *The Spirit and the Forms of Love* (1968), Williams developed his understanding of the Christian faith within the context of process thought.[6] Indeed, the latter work was credited by one reviewer as being the first systematic theology to be written from the process perspective.[7] Although Williams is normally identified as a process theologian, his

---

[3]Alfred North Whitehead, *Process and Reality* (New York: Macmillan, 1929) 532.

[4]Cobb and Griffin, *Process Theology*, 8.

[5]Ibid., 178.

[6]References to these books will be given in the text with the following abbreviations:

GG *God's Grace and Man's Hope* (New York: Harper & Brothers, 1949)
SFL *The Spirit and the Forms of Love* (New York: Harper & Row, 1968).

A bibliography of Williams's works appeared in *Union Seminary Quarterly Review* 30 (Winter-Summer 1975): 217-29.

[7]John B. Cobb, Jr., "A Process Systematic Theology," *Journal of Religion* 50 (April 1970): 199.

theological and philosophical background is quite diverse and ec-lectic. In many ways he is a mediating theologian because of his willingness to draw insights from several traditions. Although he draws heavily from the thought of Whitehead and Hartshorne, he rarely discusses the fine points of process philosophy and gener-ally avoids the sophisticated process terminology. For this reason his thought will be more easily presented to the nonspecialist. Be-sides process thought, Williams reflects the concerns of "empirical theology" at the University of Chicago.[8] His familiarity with the broad spectrum of contemporary theology is especially clear in *What Present Day Theologians Are Thinking*. In this chapter I will highlight the influence of process thought on his affirmation of divine suf-fering, at the same time recognizing that Williams has other inter-ests.

PROCESS METAPHYSICS AND THE CHRISTIAN FAITH

Whitehead once described Christianity as a religion in search of a metaphysic.[9] Williams is convinced that Whitehead's own meta-physical scheme is a viable alternative as a philosophical frame-work for interpreting the Christian faith in the twentieth century. Indeed, he argues that process thought allows a recovery of many aspects of the biblical message neglected in traditional theism (*SFL* 107). Williams recognizes, however, that metaphysical systems are relatively unpopular in the twentieth century and that many theo-logians argue that philosophy distorts rather than illuminates the Bible. For these reasons Williams frequently notes the nature and purpose of metaphysics in general before arguing for the adoption of any particular metaphysic. Following Whitehead, Williams ar-gues that metaphysics consists of generalizations about reality based on human experience (*SFL* 9). Metaphysical concepts are

---

[8]Bernard E. Meland, ed., *The Future of Empirical Theology* (Chicago: University of Chicago Press, 1969) 45-47, discusses Williams's place in this tradition.

[9]Alfred North Whitehead, *Religion in the Making* (New York: World Publishing Co., 1960) 50.

valid to the extent that they fit experience and cohere with each other.[10] Whitehead's view of metaphysics is much more modest than Hegel's, for example, and Whitehead rejects the claim to finality for any philosophy, including his own.[11] Metaphysics is a necessary component of philosophy; Whitehead and Williams reject the contemporary temptation to reduce philosophy to linguistic or phenomenological analysis.

Williams argues that process philosophy is the most viable context for interpreting the Christian faith in our time. Although he occasionally criticizes Whitehead's scheme, he basically follows it while acknowledging a certain debt to Hartshorne's views. Before moving to Williams's understanding of God's relation to the world, I must give some attention to the general tenets of process thought. Williams rarely uses the technical jargon of Whiteheadian thought, but he frequently summarizes process thought for the lay reader.[12] In general, Whitehead's philosophy is one of organism: the world is seen as a complex society of real things interacting with each other. Reality consists of events undergoing processes of becoming. Each event responds to the past by a feeling reaction and to the future by way of anticipation. Whitehead criticizes much of classical philosophy for its preoccupation with the static aspects of reality. Process philosophy, by contrast, stresses development, becoming, flux, and the temporal dimension of reality. Organic interrelatedness is intrinsic to all of reality. Events are related to each other by feelings or "prehensions." All finite reality interacts within

---

[10]See Daniel Day Williams, "Deity, Monarchy, and Metaphysics: Whitehead's Critique of the Theological Tradition," in Ivor Leclerc, ed., *The Relevance of Whitehead* (New York: Macmillan, 1961) 359-61; "How Does God Act?: An Essay in Whitehead's Metaphysics," in William L. Reese and Eugene Freeman, eds., *Process and Divinity* (LaSalle IL: Open Court, 1964) 163-64.

[11]Daniel Day Williams, "Philosophy and Faith: A Study in Hegel and Whitehead," in John Deschner, Leroy T. Howe, and Klaus Penzel, eds., *Our Common History as Christians* (New York: Oxford University Press, 1975) 164.

[12]Williams, "How Does God Act?" 164-70; "God and Time," *South East Asia Journal of Theology* 2 (January 1961): 14-15; *SFL* 102-10.

the context of possibilities Whitehead calls "eternal objects." These too are prehended by finite reality. Although Whitehead does not attribute conscious volition and awareness to all levels of reality, he does argue that feeling characterizes all of reality. Williams notes: "To be anything is to be an active functioning reality entering into dynamic relations with other things" (*GG* 41-42). In addition, process thought allows for considerable freedom and novelty in the universe.

GOD AND THE WORLD

Williams adopts Whitehead's metaphysical scheme primarily because of the emphasis on God interacting with the world. "This philosophy makes it possible for the Living God, the God who acts, the caring, saving God of the Bible to be made intelligible" (*GG* 42). Process theology uses Whiteheadian philosophy to illuminate and interpret the biblical message and to criticize several aspects of classical Christian theism. In this section I will sketch out Williams's process understanding of God's relation to the world. In the next section the process critique of classical theism will be developed.

According to Whitehead, God must exemplify the metaphysical scheme rather than be an exception to it.[13] In a sense Whitehead is pushing the analogy-of-being tradition of classical theism more radically and consistently than medieval theology did.[14] The categories that fit finite reality as we know it should be applicable to the supreme reality, God. Whitehead and Williams will occasionally grant an exception for God, but generally metaphysical concepts should apply to God as well as to the finite world. Before Williams develops the dynamics of God's relation to the world, he notes several general features of Whitehead's view of God.[15] First, God is not the sole cause of all events. God does not cause events to happen; process thought does not allow for divine determin-

---

[13]Whitehead, *Process and Reality*, 521.

[14]Williams, "God and Time," 15.

[15]Williams, "How Does God Act?" 170-71.

ism. Second, God's actions must not violate the metaphysical scheme. This scheme is part of his essence, and God could not contradict his own nature. Third, God feels or prehends the world, so there is interaction between God and the world: God is aware of mankind and mankind is aware of God. Fourth, causality is complex and includes, for example, final causation, self-causation, and efficient causation. Fifth, God's action does differ from creaturely action due to his metaphysical status.

The process God is dipolar, manifesting both a primordial nature and a consequent nature. These two poles are not two distinct beings or natures, but they are different facets of God's nature. God's primordial nature "is his envisagement of the realm of possibility in its abstraction from all particular matters of fact."[16] In his primordial nature God influences the world by "being" rather than "acting." "He is the order upon which everything existing must draw if it is to be at all. The primordial nature simply is what it is and nothing can be anything in particular without prehending that order."[17] In other words, the primordial nature acts as a lure for the world by presenting the relevant realm of possibilities for finite reality. God moves the world without being moved. This aspect of God is eternal, unchanging, and somewhat like Aristotle's unmoved mover. This aspect has all of the traditional attributes for God that a classical theist might want to use. "It is eternal, it cannot be acted upon, it cannot suffer" (*SFL* 108). The primordial nature does not, however, determine the course of finite history. It moves the world by luring or persuasion rather than coercion. The world can reject, accept, or modify the lure offered by God.

On the other side, God's consequent nature is temporal and changing. It is "consequent on the conditions presented to God by the world."[18] God receives from the world; he is acted upon as well as acting. God is passive as well as active. The events of the world make a difference to God. This consequent nature can then act on

---

[16]Ibid., 171.

[17]Ibid.

[18]Williams, "God and Time," 15.

the world in light of its perception of the world.[19] God's consequent nature responds to the concrete situation of the world,
whereas the primordial nature sets the ultimate range of possibilities before the world. The world experiences God's consequent
nature as well as his primordial nature.

Williams suggests three consequences of this process metaphysic. First, it allows for the reality of freedom and time within
human history. God does not negate time or eliminate finite freedom. "God holds the world together by offering his eternal structure of value to every particular experience so that everything
happens in significant relation to the world order and the community of beings. But God's function as cosmic orderer does not
destroy the freedom of the creatures within the order" (*SFL* 109).
Williams suggests that Whitehead may have replaced the absolute
monarch of classical theism with a constitutional monarch.[20] We
will soon see that Williams may want God to be more powerful or
directive in his governing of the world than Whitehead allows.
Second, Williams notes that process theology takes the problem of
evil seriously, but God is not made the sole cause for the world's
suffering. Third, process theology provides a new understanding
of human and divine love. These last two consequences will be developed in a later section of this chapter.

PROCESS THEOLOGY AND CLASSICAL THEISM

Process theologians have frequently criticized classical Christian theism for its understanding of God. Following Whitehead and
others, Williams joins this critical chorus and argues that process
theology can recover some valuable insights into God's nature.
Traditionally God has been pictured as a divine monarch or despot
who is static, unchanging, and controls the world totally. Whitehead argues that in Christian theology there are three strains of

---

[19]In a few places Whitehead refers to a "superjective" aspect of God,
which is primarily the effect of his consequent nature on the world. See,
for example, *Process and Reality*, 134-35.

[20]Williams, "Deity, Monarchy, and Metaphysics," 368.

thought: "God in the image of an imperial ruler, God in the image of a personification of moral energy, God in the image of an ultimate philosophical principle."[21] These three strains correspond to the mind-sets of the Roman caesars, the Hebrew Prophets, and Aristotle's unmoved mover. In early Christian history theologians attributed to God, for example, the characteristics of tyrants. Whitehead insisted that a better, more moral view of God was available in the Gospels and the philosophy of Plato.[22] Plato noted that God operated by persuasion rather than coercion, and a similar insight into God's power is found in the life of Christ. Williams argues that Whitehead did not stress enough his *moral* protest against classical theism. Although Whitehead tends to highlight aesthetic categories, "implicit within them is his appeal to moral intuition. It is here that the most important element in his protest against the divine Monarch appears. Whitehead's argument is that theological doctrine has lagged behind the fundamental ethical intuition both of Plato and of the Gospel itself."[23] He notes that Whitehead developed an ethical theism that criticized Christianity for not adequately building on its own moral insights.

Williams's critique of traditional theology focuses frequently on the synthesis of Neoplatonic philosophy with the Christian faith, especially as this synthesis was crystallized in Augustine. This synthesis has haunted Christian thought about God for centuries. The process critique of classical theism is so strong and sweeping that it is frequently called Neoclassical theism. Williams argues that the Christian faith was distorted by the use of Neoplatonic metaphysics to describe God. Every type of perfection was ascribed to God, such as power, eternity, knowledge. Any reference to divine temporality, change, passivity, or suffering was avoided. Divine impassibility was a logical consequence of the Neoplatonic orientation. Every theologian granted that the incarnate Son suffered in

---

[21]Whitehead, *Process and Reality*, 520.

[22]Alfred North Whitehead, *Adventures of Ideas* (New York: Macmillan, 1933) 213-17.

[23]Williams, "Deity, Monarchy, and Metaphysics," 356.

the crucifixion, but certainly the Father did not. Theologians assumed that "temporality and passivity mean[t] an inferior level of reality" (*SFL* 93). The Neoplatonic scheme helped to highlight God's sovereignty and majesty, but it did not preserve the biblical emphasis on his temporal interaction with the world. Many process theologians noted that these early theologians accented only one pole of God's dipolar nature, which resulted in a misunderstanding of God. Only when both aspects of God's nature (primordial and consequent, absolute and relative) are held in tension can one have an adequate view of God.[24] Classical theism erred in stressing only one side of God's nature.

The synthesis of Christian faith and Neoplatonism was given its definitive form by Augustine. Augustine acknowledged that God acted in history (e.g., the Incarnation), but insisted that God's eternity precluded any reference to divine passibility. Such a formulation results in several unfortunate consequences (*SFL* 95-102). First, Augustine's theology necessitates a denial of human freedom and an affirmation of predestination. Williams grants that Augustine's stress on the necessity of grace is valid, but Augustine's divine determinism rules out the possibility of human response to that grace. For Augustine, God's power is total. God's eternity and omniscience would be jeopardized if human response made a difference to God. Second, Augustine's emphasis on God's absoluteness de-emphasized the temporal and creaturely dimension. Love of the unchangeable and eternal is put on a higher plane than love of the temporal.

The Augustinian synthesis dominated Western theology for centuries. Although many disagreed with Augustine on key issues, the assumption of divine impassibility and immutability prevailed. Process thought accepts the temporal aspect of God's experience through his consequent nature. In general, process theology builds on the modern world view dominated by evolution, becoming, and temporality. Williams argues that theologians who recognize the problems of the Augustinian synthesis should

---

[24]See Charles Hartshorne, *The Divine Relativity* (New Haven: Yale University Press, 1948).

not criticize all metaphysics but should consider the process model. Many who criticize metaphysics think only in terms of schemes that stress static, unchanging Being. Process philosophy is a revolution in metaphysics and can generate a much-needed revision in theology. Indeed, process theologians claim that their world view "brings us closer to the biblical view of the creative and redemptive working of God than theology has been since the first century" (*SFL* vii).

DIVINE SENSITIVITY

Williams's understanding of God reaches its logical conclusion in his affirmation of divine suffering, "a problem that somehow will not rest in the Christian mind and conscience."[25] In almost all of his works, he alludes to the topic, and occasionally he presents the specific arguments for his position. In general, the process stress on God's involvement in the world entails divine suffering, even if that point is not explicitly asserted. I noted in the first chapter that Williams cites process philosophy, the biblical theology movement, and the new concern for the atonement as the three most crucial factors in the "structural shift in the Christian mind" toward the affirmation of divine passibility.[26] Because divine passibility is such a natural consequence of the process view, Williams does not always develop his arguments for it in a systematic fashion. My concern in this section is to show the variety of ways Williams presents his doctrine of divine suffering.

Although not a biblical specialist, Williams often notes that the Bible describes God as an active participant in history. He acknowledges, however, that he does "not know of a single text that one could invoke clearly and unequivocally to show that Scripture explicitly asserts the suffering of God."[27] Some texts imply that God

---

[25]Daniel Day Williams, "The Vulnerable and the Invulnerable God," *Christianity and Crisis* 22 (5 March 1962): 27.

[26]Daniel Day Williams, *What Present Day Theologians Are Thinking*, 3d ed., rev. (New York: Harper & Row, 1967) 172.

[27]Williams, "The Vulnerable and the Invulnerable God," 27.

is invulnerable and above the world's misery, while other texts suggest that God suffers with mankind and is vulnerable to the world. Williams's dipolar view of God allows him to keep God's vulnerability and invulnerability in tension.

Suffering and Being

One of Williams's key strategies in discussing divine suffering is to begin with a phenomenological analysis of human suffering. Once the essential structures of suffering have been established by phenomenological investigation, one can speak about the suffering of God. Williams begins by distinguishing "suffering" from "evil." "Suffering in its widest sense means being acted upon."[28] Suffering is not identical with evil and may not always entail pain. Most people who discuss suffering focus on acute suffering, which has the "character of threatening our self-direction, and, therefore, implicitly, our being."[29] Williams presents three aspects of suffering: identification, communication, and healing.

(1) Suffering may produce a heightened self-consciousness and a sense of identity that is not possible when one is not suffering. To avoid or reject suffering may ultimately lead to the loss of selfhood. Williams is almost proposing, "I suffer, therefore I am." Suffering does not guarantee a strong sense of identity, but it may be the occasion for identification and becoming. (2) Suffering as communication points to the possibility for an increased sense of community. Suffering might lead to the breakdown of community and create further isolation, but it might function creatively in the context of a community of interpretation. Suffering evokes community when it is remembered and reconceived in the present. (3) Suffering also has a healing power. When suffering is objectified in the presence of another person (e.g., in a therapy setting), healing can begin. "Part of the power of healing lies in discovering an-

---

[28]Daniel Day Williams, "Suffering and Being in Empirical Theology," *The Future of Empirical Theology*, 181.

[29]Ibid.

other who can hear my story, experience my feeling, and not be destroyed by it."[30]

If this is the essential structure of human suffering, Williams infers that God must suffer also. Williams agrees with the empirical-theology position (e.g., Wieman) that says human suffering points to divine suffering. "We experience the weaving together into one community of being . . . many strands of action, feeling, pain, language, memory, and expectation. Man is in the weaving, but he is not the weaver."[31] Williams goes beyond the empirical-theology perspective, however, by suggesting that the community of being includes God as its supreme member. He proposes modifying the traditional use of analogy in religious language by treating the "community of analogous structures."[32] Analogical language *is* appropriate for God even though it must be used with caution.

With this perspective on the three aspects of human suffering and the use of analogy, Williams concludes that God suffers. "I am affirming the doctrine of divine sensitivity. Without it I can make no sense of the history of God. Sensitive participation in this world means suffering, or else our experience is completely irrelevant to anything we can say about God."[33]

God as Love

Williams also derives much of his emphasis on divine suffering or sensitivity from an intensive analysis of love. Indeed, *The Spirit and the Forms of Love* is devoted entirely to this project, and many of his other works suggest the theme. He argues that the classic view of God as immutable and impassible makes the biblical claim that "God is love" (1 John 4:8) unintelligible (*SFL* 10). Williams notes the frequent reference to God's love in both of the testaments. In the Old Testament God was related to the Hebrews by election love

---

[30]Ibid., 188.

[31]Ibid., 190.

[32]Ibid., 191.

[33]Ibid., 192.

and covenant love. God's love for the Hebrews is described in personal terms on the basis of the parent-child or the husband-wife relationship. Although God's love is usually mentioned in the context of the covenant community, some passages imply that God loves all mankind. Many passages point to God's power and faithfulness in maintaining the covenant relationship, but some point to divine suffering as another dimension of the relationship. Williams acknowledges that the "general tendency of interpretation of the Hebraic faith seems against the idea that God suffers," but there are some clues to divine suffering (*SFL* 30). He argues with Heschel that divine pathos is central to Hebrew prophetic theology: If God loves mankind, then he suffers.

The New Testament makes the love of God central. Divine love and suffering are epitomized in the incarnation, life, and death of Jesus. Like many other contemporary theologians, Williams argues that the Christian view of God must be developed in light of the revelation of Jesus rather than from the standpoint of Greek metaphysics. Early Christology was preoccupied with the problem of two natures rather than divine love or suffering. For Williams, love necessarily entails suffering and vulnerability. "In human terms, surely, to love *is* to be vulnerable—vulnerable to the hurts and risks that come from setting the other free and accepting his freedom."[34] Besides his general sensitivity to human misery, God suffers with Christ. "As Jesus suffers in his love with and for sinners, he discloses the suffering love of God" (*SFL* 166). Here Williams opposes the traditional view that suffering is inappropriate for God: "Thus power is divine but pity is human" (*SFL* 167). Early theologians feared that any reference to divine suffering would compromise God's deity, yet Williams argues that God is both revealed and hidden in the suffering of Jesus. Although the cross of Jesus has been the subject of many atonement theories, Williams notes that most neglect God's suffering love. He suggests that Jesus' suffering both discloses God's suffering and opens up the possibility of reconciliation between God and man. "Jesus' suffering has transforming power not merely as a demonstration of a

---

[34]Williams, "The Vulnerable and the Invulnerable God," 28.

truth but as an action which creates a new field of force in which forgiven men can be changed" (*SFL* 184).

Although Williams argues for divine sensitivity, he acknowledges that impassibility was based on a partial truth. "The truth of impassibility is that God's love is the everlasting power and spirit of deity. . . . Unlimited love belongs to him as it belongs to no creature. God's love is absolute in its integrity forever. In this sense his love is invulnerable" (*SFL* 185). Despite this truth, however, the impassibility doctrine was so formulated as to jeopardize the biblical emphasis on divine love. If the Father does not suffer, Christ's suffering appears to be a price required by a callous God. If God does not suffer, then his love is so radically different from human love that it becomes unintelligible.

Besides arguing for divine sensitivity on the basis of Christology, Williams uses phenomenological analysis much as he did in relation to suffering. His strategy is to determine the essential structures of human love and draw metaphysical and theological insights from these (*SFL* 111). Just as an analysis of human suffering led to divine suffering, so an analysis of human love will lead to the doctrine of divine suffering. Williams again acknowledges that process philosophy is not proposing a total, absolute understanding of reality, but he is convinced that the structures of human experience tell us something significant about ultimate reality. Focusing on interpersonal love, Williams discerns five "categories of love": individuality, freedom, action and suffering, causality, and impartial judgment.

(1) "Love requires real individuals, unique beings, each bringing to the relationship something which no other can bring" (*SFL* 114). True love depends on individuals who build relationships without threatening the identity or selfhood of the other person. People are loved because of their unique identity, not because they fit some general type. Each person brings to the loving relationship an originality and must acknowledge the uniqueness of the other. (2) Love entails some human freedom. Loving relationships are not determined by fate yet are not wholly the result of human volition. Love always occurs within a historical context that involves risk and ambiguity. Loving is risking. Love also involves accepting the other person's freedom. To deny the other's freedom

would be to reject love. The freedom experienced in love is never total, but finite freedom is essential to human love. (3) Love entails the capacity to act and to be acted upon. Williams defines suffering as the capacity to be acted upon or changed. Suffering is not incidental to the loving relation; it is essential to it. (4) Love is meaningless if it is not causal. "Unless the actions and suffering of one move the other to action and suffering, the relationship is futile" (*SFL* 119). True love responds to the givenness of the past and to the possibilities of the future. Love's causality is not coercive. Although love always sets limits and conditions, the motivation is the well-being and growth of the beloved. Love does not mean the imposition of one's will on another. Love can cause the transformation of the other, but the other is not forced into a mold. (5) Love includes impartial judgment. Williams here criticizes the formation of a false dichotomy between love and rational, objective thought. If one is genuinely concerned about the welfare of the other person, then objective knowledge of the situation is required. "To love is to accept responsibility for assessing the real situation in which we love, and that means self-discovery and discovery of the other" (*SFL* 121). Some argue that love should be uncalculating, but true love requires a realistic appraisal of the needs of the beloved. Williams insists that love and equity are compatible and necessarily interrelated (cf. *SFL* 243-75).

Given these five categories of love, Williams attempts to characterize God. He is aware of the danger of simply projecting a human type of love onto God's character, but he is also aware that the Bible consistently portrays God as loving. There must be something in common between human love and divine love. As we noted above, Williams is willing to follow the traditional view of religious language as analogy. Williams's concern is to develop a doctrine of God based on these metaphysical-phenomenological categories of love. It is illegitimate, he argues, to assume they do not fit God. God is different from the finite world, yet these categories can illuminate God's nature. Whitehead insisted that God must exemplify the metaphysical scheme, but even there some exceptions were made. Williams comments: "The problem of a metaphysical theology is to carry through the analogy of being with full

justice both to the structures of experience and to the transmutation of structures as they apply to the being of God" (*SFL* 124).
Whitehead grants, for example, that God is necessary to each and
every finite reality, not that finite reality is absolutely necessary to
God. Williams suggests that perhaps theology would be in better
shape if it attended to the language of devotion, where God is described as loving and suffering, rather than focusing on traditional
ontological language.[35]

Based on these five categories, Williams develops the following
view of God. (1) Even traditional theology argued for the individuality of God. The doctrine of the Trinity complicates the issue, but
at least here traditional theism was forced to recognize "that an absolutely solitary individual can neither love nor be loved" (*SFL* 126).
To follow the category of individuality, God is the one who creates
the community of beings with whom he can have loving relations.
(2) If God loves mankind, he cannot predestine or determine human destiny. If God's love is anything like human love, it must involve the risk of rejection. God's love has a coercive dimension to
it, as we shall see shortly, but God does not manipulate mankind.
"If destiny is the shape of a possible future which must be actualized in freedom, then God is the supreme predestinator. Every
destiny is shaped by him. But destiny without freedom is meaningless" (*SFL* 127). (3) The suffering dimension of love necessitates
the rejection of divine impassibility. "Impassibility makes love
meaningless" (*SFL* 127). Here Williams is quite aware of the limits
of analogical God-talk. Suffering does not jeopardize God's being
or integrity, although that is the result when humans suffer. Suffering may reflect a threat to the fulfillment of God's purpose at a
particular juncture in history, but it does not pose a threat to his
being. Some human suffering is due to the limitations of knowledge. God knows all possible outcomes and the limits of tragedy.
God is invulnerable in the integrity of his being just as he is vulnerable through his love for mankind. Williams again criticizes tra-

---

[35]J. K. Mozley, *The Impassibility of God: A Survey of Christian Thought*
(Cambridge: Cambridge University Press, 1926) 6, argues that liturgical-
devotional language should be kept distinct from theological reflection.

ditional theology for artificially separating the suffering of the Son from the Father. (4) God's love is causal, but God is not the sole cause of every event. As we noted earlier, causality is complex and God's causation is frequently persuasive rather than coercive. (5) Although Williams does not deal explicitly with God and impartial judgment, the relation is self-evident. God is supremely aware of the human situation and our needs. Because of his perfect knowledge, God can respond appropriately and lovingly to that situation.

Power, Tragedy, and Hope

How does God respond to human suffering? So far we have seen Williams's emphasis on divine sensitivity and his critique of classical theism. These themes have been typical of process theology in general and reflect Williams's concern to develop a truly Christian view of God. Most Christian theists would also ask if God does anything to overcome or alleviate human suffering. It may be comforting to know God suffers with us, but how is God working to stop or reduce the suffering? On this point Williams relates a conversation with a student who had suffered intense pain for a long time without any foreseeable relief. The student remarked: "You know, the doctrine of divine impassibility is meaning more and more to me. Somewhere this suffering has got to stop."[36] Williams agrees that from the standpoint of the Christian faith, the suffering of mankind must stop if Christian hope is to have any validity at all. Instead of reviving the doctrine of divine impassibility, however, Williams argues that the vulnerable, suffering God has an invulnerable dimension also. Both dimensions derive from God's love for mankind. "The invulnerability of God is his *being* as love. . . . And it is the being of God that is invulnerable. It is his being that is the ground of everything that is. It is this divine love that remains faithful to everything he has made."[37]

---

[36]Williams, "The Vulnerable and the Invulnerable God," 29.

[37]Ibid., 30.

When Williams describes the vulnerable and invulnerable dimensions of God's love, he is generally operating within the context of Whitehead's dipolar theism. Williams modifies Whitehead's
view when he articulates God's power and involvement in the
world. Williams asks two questions of Whitehead's view of God.[38]
(1) Does Whitehead really avoid the divine-despot position of classical theism? (2) If he avoids the theist position, is his God too weak
to help suffering mankind? As he answers these questions, Williams pushes Whitehead's theology a little closer to the theist position. (1) If God provides the ultimate range of possibilities for
finite events, is he still controlling the world? Whitehead's response would be that God merely sets the limits for finite events,
but does not determine them like a despot. God acts as a lure for
finite events but not as a divine manipulator. (2) Williams then
wonders if Whitehead's God is too weak. Perhaps Whitehead
stressed the persuasive power of God to the neglect of the divine
coercive power. Perhaps Whitehead may have substituted a constitutional monarch for an arbitrary, absolute monarch. Williams
would opt for more divine initiative in human history than Whitehead suggests. Williams asks of Whitehead: "Does God only listen
or does he speak?"[39] To give more stress to divine coercion does
not necessitate a return to a barbaric, despotic view of deity; Williams argues that more divine coercion is justified by an analysis of
religious experience.[40] Whitehead reacted so strongly against the
view of God as an arbitrary monarch that he neglected the divine
initiative in history.

Going beyond the question of divine power, Williams devotes
considerable attention to the way in which God transmutes human suffering and eventually alleviates it. Although he does not
develop a full-fledged process eschatology, he is concerned to describe how God will overcome human tragedy. Here again Williams is apparently modifying Whitehead's position. Whitehead left

---

[38]Williams, "Deity, Monarchy, and Metaphysics," 365.

[39]Ibid., 368.

[40]Ibid., 370.

the future more open-ended than Williams's theological stance will allow. Although not a Hegelian, Williams does note that Hegel's theology was more definite about God's final victory over evil than is Whitehead's.[41] In addition, Williams clearly opposes the contemporary attitude that human suffering is unending. He calls this form of resignation the "Beckett effect" because of Samuel Beckett's apparent despair about the human situation.[42] The Christian faith interpreted within the context of process philosophy can be confident of God's eventual victory over human suffering. Although God suffers, he is not weak. "Suffering in the being of God is not just any suffering; it is the supreme instance of the transmutation of suffering."[43]

Williams, like most process theologians, is sensitive to the criticism of process theodicy. Many critics have taken the process emphasis on divine persuasion as an open admission that God cannot ultimately help suffering mankind. Madden and Hare, for example, claim that given the amount and distribution of suffering in the world, Whitehead's God seems to be a very ineffective persuader. Using the analogy of the leader of an organization, they point to two difficulties with the process scheme.[44] First, there have been many cases of human cooperation for the sake of a good cause, but there has been little success. Second, the amount of existing evil is evidence against a persuasive power for God. Apparently God is not a very effective persuader and is unable to alleviate human suffering. Indeed, the evidence could just as plausibly support the view that an evil persuader is at work. Cases of good, moral behavior may actually be evidence of resistance to the evil, per-

---

[41]Williams, "Philosophy and Faith," 168.

[42]Williams, "Suffering and Being in Empirical Theology," 193. Williams grants that Beckett may have some hope for the future, but here Williams is depicting the impression that one gets from Beckett's dramas.

[43]Ibid., 192.

[44]Edward H. Madden and Peter H. Hare, *Evil and the Concept of God* (Springfield IL: Charles C. Thomas, 1968) 121-22. For a good response to Madden and Hare, see Lewis S. Ford, "Divine Persuasion and the Triumph of the Good," *Process Philosophy and Christian Thought*, 283-304.

suasive power.[45] By introducing more coercive power into his description of God, Williams has partially avoided the charge. My concern here is to show how Williams's God transmutes suffering in the present; for this, I will need to sketch Williams's theology of history and eschatology.

God's response to evil constitutes a four-stage "divine strategy of redemption" (*GG* 53-57). First, God responds to "intolerable evil" with his wrath. Divine wrath is redemptive, says Williams, rather than vengeful. God has so created the world that certain consequences, often painful, follow from certain actions. Indirectly, then, God through his created order may be the cause of some suffering. Second, "God's redemption means the transmutation of evil and loss into new good, and higher fulfillment" (*GG* 54). Williams does not generalize that all evil will be transformed into good, but in principle God can bring good out of evil. Third, God offers forgiveness to every person. This forgiveness has been mediated to human history through Jesus. Fourth, God preserves the past for succeeding generations. "God's love does not change. But the 'career' of His love in His dealing with the world involves a continual sifting of the evil from the good, a creative thrust toward a more complete exemplification of His good in existence, and, it is possible to believe, a treasuring for all time of the good which does come to be" (*GG* 57).

Williams perceives his process position to be a synthesis of the best insights of Protestant liberalism and neo-orthodoxy about God's involvement in history. In general he sees liberalism leaning too far toward optimism and neo-orthodoxy leaning too far toward pessimism. Christ brought about the decisive defeat of the forces of evil, but suffering will continue until the end of time as we know it (*GG* 129-34). History is not a continual progress toward the Kingdom of God, but there is a real basis for hope because of God's action in Christ. The Christian can be confident of the outcome of history, but the battles of the present are real. A creative and re-

---

[45]Peter H. Hare and Edward H. Madden, "Evil and Persuasive Power," *Process Studies* 2 (Spring 1972): 47.

demptive power was released by Christ, but the ultimate resolution of suffering is eschatological.

When Williams treats the eschatological dimension of theodicy, he recognizes that the Bible never presents a systematic, uniform witness. The Bible includes a variety of eschatological symbols, each of which is rooted in God's redemptive activity in history. Hence Williams defines eschatology as "an anticipation of last things on the basis of God's self-revelation of his ultimate will and character in actual history."[46] Out of all these eschatological symbols, Williams frequently cites the imagery of 1 Corinthians 15:25: "For he must reign until he has put all his enemies under his feet" (RSV). Despite this eschatological hope, Williams acknowledges the reality of evil and the tragic dimension of human existence. Williams is confident that the divine resources are sufficient to transmute evil into good. However, he refuses to speculate about the exact course of history and the meaning of eschatological symbols. He realizes that some will object that his eschatology is not strong enough for hope about the future. He responds that he is basing what "might be" on "what is" (i.e., God's action in history, especially in Christ) rather than on speculation.[47] Nevertheless, Williams expresses clearly that his eschatology allows for the possibility of ultimate loss. Because of human freedom, there can be conflict between creator and creature. Hence human loss can be tragic and real. Despite the universalistic passages in the New Testament and God's intention that all respond favorably to his persuasion, final loss is a possibility when human freedom is real. God does not send anyone to hell directly, but hell is a possibility. "There may be irrevocable hells to which men in their freedom drive themselves; but they are irrevocable because of what men decide, not because of the will of a merciful God."[48] Although he always notes the resources of divine love and mercy, Williams will not preclude human freedom and the possibility of tragedy.

---

[46]Daniel Day Williams, "Tragedy and the Christian Eschatology," *Encounter* 24 (Winter 1963): 68.

[47]Ibid., 76.

[48]Ibid., 75.

Although our interest in Williams's thought has been with his view of God, his ethical position bears directly on the theodicy issue. God suffers with mankind and transmutes suffering, but some of the responsibility for alleviating human suffering falls to man. I cannot develop Williams's ethic in any detail here, except to stress that human activity is crucial to his theodicy. As I noted earlier, Williams suggests that a process view of history is more valid than the unrealistic pessimism of neo-orthodoxy or the impractical optimism of liberalism and the social gospel. His perspective is based on two basic convictions (*GG* 11). First, he agrees with liberalism that the world can be made better through human effort. Second, he agrees with neo-orthodoxy that any genuine hope cannot be grounded in human activity alone. God's initiative is decisive. "To try to establish the City of Man on anything other than faith in God is to build on quicksand" (*GG* 11). Although mankind will never be able to establish the Kingdom of God on earth, Williams insists that a process view of God, including his suffering love, can be the foundation for action to alleviate human misery. Williams's thesis is this: *"The living God whose nature and purpose is love calls us to respond in our freedom to the tasks which are set for us by the fact that He is at work in our human history both as Creator and Redeemer"* (*GG* 147). The ideal Christian response to this living, loving God is Christian action. Because God is acting in human history, so Christians can and should work to establish a better world. Christian hope about human history is characterized by three attitudes. First, it is *"sustained by, and expresses itself in, a reverent grateful love for the good earth"* (*GG* 163). Williams's concern for the "good earth" and the natural environment reflects the process interest in subhuman as well as human destiny.[49] Second, Christian hope is sustained by and expressed in the constant effort to create the "Good Society." Here Williams avoids the extreme of utopianism but argues for the possibility of a better, more humane life for all. Third, Christian hope is based on faith in the Kingdom of God. No human society can be identified with the Kingdom of God, yet the Kingdom can func-

---

[49]For another expression of the process concern with ecology, see John B. Cobb, Jr., *Is It Too Late? A Theology of Ecology* (Encino CA: Glencoe, 1971).

tion as an ideal to spur further Christian action. Overall, Williams's stress on divine sensitivity is matched by a concern for human sensitivity to the suffering of other human beings. A God who is caring and suffering calls forth a sympathetic human response.

DIVINE DESPOT, DIVINE AESTHETE, OR DIVINE COMPANION?

Process philosophy and theology have provoked widespread interest and criticism. No attempt will be made here to offer a systematic critique of process thought in general or of Daniel Day Williams in particular. Several aspects of Williams's doctrine of divine sensitivity deserve attention, but my concern here is to focus on one issue: how does God's suffering help the human sufferer? My approach will be to isolate three images for God suggested by Williams in his discussion: divine despot, divine aesthete, and divine companion. Williams clearly opts for the third image; his reasons for rejecting the other two, especially the second, require fuller clarification.

Williams, like Whitehead, rejects the concept of God as divine despot. God does not determine human history through any prearranged plan or the use of coercive power. Rather, God offers ideal aims to finite reality and allows for free response to those aims. God is not the only cause in the universe and is not directly responsible for human suffering. The divine-monarch view is a distortion of the best insights of the Bible and human experience. Williams modified Whitehead's view of divine power in order to allow for divine coercion to work in tandem with divine persuasion. God still does not control or manipulate the world, but Williams points to more divine initiative in history than Whitehead seems to allow. Like other process theologians, Williams recognizes that religious experience is often evoked by an awareness of divine power. The mistake of classical theists has been what David Ray Griffin calls the "omnipotence fallacy"—the belief that all con-

ceivable power must be attributed to God.[50] God's power is meaningless, however, if there are not other beings with some degree
of power who can interact with the divine power. Williams wants
to preserve the emphasis on divine initiative highlighted by the divine-despot proponents, but he insists on the need for human
freedom as well.

Although I find Williams's critique of the divine-despot model
cogent, he probably would win more converts from that camp if he
had dealt more extensively with biblical texts supportive of his position. Just as few texts unequivocally support divine suffering, so
few texts unequivocally support his emphasis on divine persuasion. Williams's exegetical gap may be typical of much of the early
history of process theology. Process theologians have tended to focus on theological and philosophical reasons for their views, but
until recently they have not developed a strong exegetical base for
their viewpoints.[51] I am confident such an exegetical base is available, but few process theologians, including Williams, have located it so far.

Williams also rejects the divine-aesthete image for God. This
view is a possible interpretation of Whitehead's theology based on
the prevalence of aesthetic categories in Whitehead's system.[52]
Stephen Ely, for example, has noted that when God feels the suffering of the world, he complements that suffering with other feelings so that God's enjoyment is complete. Ely suggests that "it is
not likely to give anyone much comfort to know that, no matter
what happens in this world, God can see it in an ideal setting that
makes it an enjoyable sight."[53] According to Ely, evil really dis-

---

[50]Griffin, God, Power, and Evil, 261-74.

[51]For recent examples of process exegesis, see ibid., 31-37; Lewis S.
Ford, The Lure of God: A Biblical Background for Process Theism (Philadel-
phia: Fortress Press, 1978); Journal of the American Academy of Religion 47
(March 1979).

[52]Whitehead, Religion in the Making, 101, is a good example.

[53]Stephen L. Ely, The Religious Availability of Whitehead's God: A Critical
Analysis (Madison: University of Wisconsin Press, 1942) 41. For a good response, see Bernard M. Loomer, "Ely on Whitehead's God," Process Philosophy and Christian Thought, 264-86.

appears as far as God is concerned. Evil remains in the world itself, but the evil is absorbed into God's comprehensive knowledge so that it is transmuted in God. If such an interpretation is accurate, Williams grants that Whitehead would be guilty of changing the divine despot into the divine aesthete. God's satisfaction would be constantly intense so that no particular complex of events will alter that feeling. Although Williams does not delve into the intricacies of Whiteheadian jargon to respond to the divine-aesthete view, it is clear that he finds a basic flaw in it. God does feel the world intensely at all times and complements his feelings of suffering with other feelings. He seems to agree with Christian's suggestion that "the *qualitative pattern* of God's satisfaction varies with the advance of nature while the intensity of his satisfaction is invariant."[54] It would seem, then, that God is always feeling the world at full intensity, but the type of feeling (grief, joy, etc.) corresponds to the feeling of the object. If we are suffering, then God suffers even though his response to that suffering transmutes it. Williams further insists that even though God transmutes this suffering with complementary feelings, he preserves the tragic dimension. He cites Whitehead's comment that "peace is the understanding of tragedy and at the same time its preservation."[55] The world's suffering does have meaning for God, Williams argues, and to suggest that God is somehow oblivious to human misery is to overlook Whitehead's strong emphasis on the consequent nature of God. God's transmutation of suffering affects the world; it does not occur merely in a transcendent realm. Ely, for example, suggests that "perhaps World Wars are the black spots necessary for the perfection of the divine painting."[56] Williams's response would be that God grieves over the destruction wrought by wars and offers ideals to mankind designed to change the course of history if accepted. Whether or not Whitehead's God comes too close to being the divine aesthete, Williams emphasizes the high moral character

[54]Williams, "Deity, Monarchy, and Metaphysics," 372.

[55]Whitehead, *Adventures of Ideas*, 368.

[56]Ely, *Religious Availability*, 51.

of God so consistently that he avoids this position. As I mentioned earlier, Williams contends that Whitehead's main critique of the divine-despot view is a moral one. If this is correct, Williams would use an ethical theism to refute the divine-aesthete charge.

Williams's position is the third option, that God is the divine companion. Like all process theologians, he is fond of quoting Whitehead's dictum that God is "the fellow-sufferer who understands."[57] Williams's emphasis on divine suffering is a key ingredient in a larger vision of how God relates to human suffering. God interacts with the world as a dipolar being. God is invulnerable to human pain insofar as his primordial nature is abstract, eternal, and unchanging. God is vulnerable to human pain insofar as his consequent nature is sensitive, temporal, and passible. In his reaction against classical theism, Williams has tended to emphasize the vulnerable dimension of God's nature.

Overall, Williams's doctrine of the divine companion is a much more attractive theological alternative than the divine despot or the divine aesthete. The divine-despot view holds that God is ultimately responsible for human suffering. Although this God has all the coercive power necessary to work miracles to alleviate human suffering, Williams is suspicious of this God's moral character. If this God caused the suffering in the first place, why would he want to eliminate it? Williams insists that Whitehead's critique of the divine despot is founded on an ethical criterion. The divine despot could help suffering humanity, but his character is called into question because he caused the suffering. The divine-aesthete view is also rejected by Williams because of God's lack of concern for the condition of the world. The divine companion responds with suffering love to human misery and acts to alleviate it. According to Williams, such a view is closer to the biblical witness, human experience, and process metaphysics. God suffers with us; he acts in the world to overcome our suffering; and he lures us to cooperate in the alleviation of suffering.

---

[57]Whitehead, *Process and Reality*, 532.

Chapter Seven

Jung Young Lee:
Divine Empathy

When J. K. Mozley wrote his historical survey of the doctrine of divine impassibility in 1926, he noted that he could find only two works specifically devoted to the topic: Gregory Thaumaturgus's *De passibili et impassibili in Deo* from the third century and Marshall Randles's *The Blessed God* from the end of the nineteenth century.[1] Although we are discussing six proponents of divine passibility in this study, only two have devoted entire books to the topic: Kazoh Kitamori's *Theology of the Pain of God* and Jung Young Lee's *God Suffers for Us*.[2] Both Kitamori and Lee have Oriental backgrounds, and both argue that their non-Western perspective helps them see the viability of divine passibility. Born in Korea in 1935, Lee was educated in the United States, receiving a Th.D. in systematic theology from Boston University in 1968. He has taught in Korea and the United States.

---

[1] J. K. Mozley, *The Impassibility of God: A Survey of Christian Thought* (London: Cambridge University Press, 1926) viii.

[2] The following abbreviations will be used for references in the text:

CR *Cosmic Religion* (New York: Harper & Row, 1978; original, Philosophical Library, 1973)

GS *God Suffers for Us: A Systematic Inquiry into a Concept of Divine Passibility* (The Hague: Martinus Nijhoff, 1974)

TC *The Theology of Change: A Christian Concept of God in an Eastern Perspective* (Maryknoll NY: Orbis Books, 1979).

A prolific writer, Lee has treated the suffering of God in many of his works. Lee's primary text, *God Suffers for Us*, is based on his doctoral dissertation at Boston University. Since that time Lee has begun to develop a sweeping interpretation of the Christian faith in light of Eastern thought, especially the metaphysics of the *I ching*.[3] Lee rarely refers to the *I ching* in *God Suffers for Us*, citing mainly Western authors. There he derives divine passibility primarily from God's loving (*agape*) nature. In his later works, however, divine passibility appears to be the logical conclusion of an Oriental metaphysic. Although my main concern is with Lee's earlier monograph, I will begin by sketching his overall theological program, especially as it is presented in his later book, *The Theology of Change* (1979).

GOD AND THE *I CHING*

Lee does not propose a specifically Korean theology. We saw earlier that Kazoh Kitamori was a strong supporter of developing a Japanese interpretation of the Christian faith. Lee would presumably favor this indigenization of the Christian faith to his native Korea, but his concern is broader. He proposes an Eastern understanding of God based on the *I ching*, a text widely revered in the Orient. Although Lee's program is not specifically Korean, his interest in demonstrating the compatibility of Christianity and Eastern culture is a strong one in recent Korean theology.[4] He argues, like Kitamori, that Christian theology was too heavily influenced by the Hellenistic perspective in the first centuries (*TC* 11-13). Valuable aspects of the Christian faith can be regained by ex-

---

[3]Some of Lee's writings on the *I ching* include: *The Principle of Changes: Understanding the* I ching (Secaucus NJ: University Books, 1971); *Death and Beyond in the Eastern Perspective: A Study Based on the Bardo Thoedol and the* I Ching (New York: Gordon and Breach, 1974); *The* I Ching *and Modern Man: Essays on Metaphysical Implications of Change* (Secaucus NJ: University Books, 1975); *Patterns of Inner Process: The Rediscovery of Jesus' Teachings in the* I Ching *and Preston Herald* (Secaucus NJ: Citadel Press, 1976).

[4]Gerald H. Anderson, ed., *Asian Voices in Christian Theology* (Maryknoll NY: Orbis Books, 1976) 170-73.

amining its relation to Eastern thought. By living in the United States and writing in English primarily, Lee has become a strong apologist for the compatibility of Christianity and Eastern thought.[5]

In his later work Lee develops a typology of theologies as the context for his theological program. The three main options in Christian theology today are the theology of the absolute, process theology, and the theology of change (*TC* 19). The theology of the absolute is Lee's rubric for almost all forms of Western theology. These theologians generally understand God via the static concept of "being" inherited ultimately from Greek philosophy. Although some contemporary theologians (neo-orthodox, death of God, theology of hope) have understood God with a more dynamic model, they do not break radically from the static Greek metaphysic.[6] Although I will refer to Lee's critique of the theology of the absolute several times, one aspect is especially central to his argument. Western thought in general, he argues, has been captivated by "either-or" thinking. It tends to stress dichotomy and discontinuity so rigidly that the interdependence and interrelation of all reality is obscured. "The dominant issue in the history of Christian thought is neither the problem of the divine reality nor that of human belief but the Western way of thinking, that is, thinking in terms of 'either/or.' "[7] This perspective distorts the Christian faith by its failure to allow for continuity. Lee proposes "both-and" thinking as a better context for interpreting the Christian faith. Western thought prefers exclusive, absolute categories. Such a view of logic is epitomized in Aristotle, Euclid, and Newton. For example, "Aristotelian 'either-or' logic presupposes an absolutely dualistic worldview, which is contradicted by the idea

---

[5]Despite Lee's apologetic efforts, he has received little critical attention outside of book reviews.

[6]Lee generally cites Moltmann's *Theology of Hope* as typical of this movement, but he ignores the later work of Moltmann, where his break with Greek metaphysics is even more pronounced (e.g., *The Crucified God*).

[7]Jung Young Lee, "The Yin-Yang Way of Thinking: A Possible Method for Ecumenical Theology," *International Review of Missions* 60 (July 1971): 363.

of mutual interdependency" (*TC* 16). Christian theology will be better served, Lee claims, by the both-and thinking of Eastern thought.

Process theology is for Lee a transitional type of theology. It stands midway between the theology of the absolute and Lee's own theology of change. Process theology has correctly broken with the dominant Western view of God as static, unchanging, eternal, and impassible. Its world view is compatible with both Western and Eastern thought. Process theology is not totally adequate, however, and Lee notes several significant differences from his own theology of change. Process theology presupposes a linear view of time, whereas Lee's view of time is cyclical (*TC* 13-14). Moreover, the two theologies see creativity differently. Process thought takes creativity to be an ultimate reality, but Lee argues that change is more basic to reality than creativity. Process theology suggests that novelty and change derive from creativity, but Lee wants to reverse the priority (*TC* 14-15). Lee also argues that process theology is not totally free from the either-or form of logic. Whitehead's God is dipolar, indicating a recognition of the both-and way of thinking, but Whitehead does not adequately stress the interrelation of the primordial and consequent natures (*TC* 17-18).

Lee offers the theology of change as a valid alternative to the theology of the absolute and process theology. Lee's theology is based on the metaphysics of the *I ching*, or *Book of Changes*, which is a Confucian classic popular in Korea, China, and Japan. For Lee the *I ching* epitomizes the Eastern mind, having an influence on the East similar to Greek philosophy's influence on the West. "If, as Whitehead remarked, all western philosophies are only footnotes to Plato, most East Asian philosophies could be called, by analogy, only commentaries on the *I ching*" (*TC* 2). Lee is convinced that the metaphysical system of the *I ching* is compatible with the contemporary Western world view and the Christian faith. Since the Christian faith has been interpreted via a variety of metaphysical systems (e.g., Plato, Aristotle, Kant, Descartes, Hegel), the metaphysics of the *I ching* should be considered as a viable alternative. The *I ching* is the classic (*ching*) of change (*i*) and argues that change is the fundamental characteristic of reality. This change is interpreted through two complementary principles, yin and yang. I shall not try to explore the intricacies of the *I ching's* world, but the yin-yang polarity is crucial to Lee's argument and deserves some clarification. Yin and yang are two primordial forces that pervade all of reality. The yin principle is symbolized by femaleness, receptivity, cold, north, earth, darkness, rest, and being. The yang principle is characterized by maleness, creativity, warmth, south, heaven, light, movement, and becoming. The mutual inclusiveness of yin and yang is symbolized by the white dot (yang) in the dark area (yin) and the dark dot (yin) in the white area (yang) (*TC* 126).

Yin and yang are manifestations of one essence, change. They are not a duality, because "the distinctions between them are conditional and existential, not essential. *Yin* and *yang* are one in essence but two in existence" (*TC* 5). The *I ching* develops the metaphysics of change through a series of duograms, trigrams, and hexagrams. In these drawings yin is represented by a broken line (- -) and yang by an unbroken line(—). The pictures include all of the possible combinations of yin and yang. The sixty-four hexagrams that result epitomize this entire metaphysical system and all of reality. Thus "to know the *I ching* is to know the universe" (*TC* 8).

The theology of change, argues Lee, is a valid interpretation of the Christian faith for three reasons (*TC* 20-26). First, it is an ecumenical theology. The theology of change operates with both-and thinking rather then either-or thought. Christianity has traditionally been presented as an exclusive religion that stressed the need for conversion, but its original message was inclusive. Christianity "can encompass all existing religions, because it encompasses the complementarity of all opposites and concrescent poles for the integration of the whole" (*TC* 21). Christianity should accent cooperation and coordination rather than competition and domination. Christianity should be a cosmic religion. Western Christianity has failed to maintain the universality of its faith (*CR* 9-10). Second, the theology of change is relevant to the contemporary world view. Lee suggests that the traditional Western world view was until recently mechanistic, materialistic, and deterministic. In light of contemporary scientific theory (e.g., Einstein's relativity theory), people see the world in more dynamic terms. Lee recognizes the danger of basing a theology on a particular world view, but he insists theology cannot be developed in a vacuum. Third, Lee's theology is a theology of ecology.[8] Traditional Christian theology was too dualistic and differentiated human beings too much from other forms of reality. The misuse of the natural world has been a frequent consequence of exalting man's status in the world (*CR* 9).

Lee treats several crucial theological topics in light of the theology of change. My plan is to sketch out his general understanding of God before turning to his arguments for divine suffering. If change characterizes all of reality, then God is best understood as "change itself." This view of God is better, Lee claims, than God as "being itself" (theology of the absolute) or "becoming itself" (process theology). Change itself is ultimately beyond human comprehension, but it can be known in its concrete, relative manifestations (*CR* 16-17). The Judeo-Christian tradition has used a variety of symbols to describe God (lord, father, creator, king, etc.), but the "primordial idea of God" is compatible with change itself (*TC* 30). Here Lee primarily uses Moses' experience with God at the burning bush and the revelation of God's name (Exodus 3:1-15). God describes himself as YHWH (Yahweh) or "I am who I am."

---

[8]Ibid., 364-65.

Lee suggests that God's name is highly ambiguous and points to the impossibility of defining God. Ultimately God is nameless and transcends any human categorization. The nonsymbolic nature of God is also recognized in the Eastern religions. For example, in Hinduism Brahman is always described with the double negation *neti, neti* ("neither this nor that") because he is incomprehensible. The nonsymbolic nature of nirvana in Buddhist thought may have some point of contact with the Judeo-Christian view of God, even though nirvana refers to an experience rather than God.

With his description of God as change itself, Lee is trying to preserve the dynamic character of God. God may also be characterized as "is-ness" itself if one recalls the dynamic connotation. He is careful to distinguish is-ness itself from Paul Tillich's view of God as being itself. Is-ness itself stresses the dynamic dimension of God while being itself stresses the "structural form of his existence" (*TC* 35). Lee insists that Exodus 3 emphasizes the dynamic character of God rather than the ontological structure of being. Yahweh refers primarily to power or energy, and El, another Hebrew name for God, means "to be strong" or "to be mighty" (*TC* 37). In this context Lee suggests an interesting analogy for God. God as is-ness is like the axis of a moving wheel. The moving is the universe. God moves the wheel as he moves; he is the "moving mover" or the "changing changer" instead of the unmoved mover of Aristotle.

Lee recognizes that his emphasis on God as change will raise questions about the traditional doctrine of God as immutable or unchanging. The real motive behind the immutability doctrine was to stress God's faithfulness in his relationships. If God is change itself, can he be trusted? Lee responds that change itself is changeless in the sense that God's change is constant and unceasing. In terms of his moral character, changelessness is God's faithfulness to himself (*TC* 43-44). The world changes because God changes, and God is totally immersed in the process of change. "God as change itself is, then, eternal change and the heart of change" (*TC* 45).

Because of God's nonsymbolic nature, he cannot be described adequately by any human concepts. Given the limits of human language, Lee proposes that both-and thinking is more appropriate than either-or thought. God manifests himself in a dipolar pro-

cess, operating through the yin and yang forces (*TC* 49; *CR* 18).
Both-and thinking can account for this manifestation and fits the
best insights of the Judeo-Christian heritage about God. Lee is particularly concerned with the prevalence of personal categories in
the traditional descriptions of God. "According to the 'both-and'
way of thinking God cannot be *either* personal *or* impersonal. God
must be *both* personal *and* impersonal" (*TC* 50). Lee notes that despite the predominance of personalistic descriptions of God, some
concepts are impersonal in that tradition. The notion of God as
Word (*logos*) is more impersonal than personal, and Hebrew names
for God such as Yahweh and Elohim originally referred to impersonal, natural forces (e.g., lightning, mountains, rivers). Lee concludes that the originally impersonal concept of God became
personalized primarily through the Exodus experience. In the Ex-
odus-Sinai events God was experienced as a magician, warrior-
king, and legislator-king. Lee also allows that this personalistic description of God may be due to the inability of human beings to
conceive of God except as a person.[9]

One of the real problems resulting from the reliance on personalistic descriptions of God is the assumption of a qualitative distinction between personal and impersonal reality, especially
between man and the natural world. Another tragic consequence
of seeing God as exclusively personal is the use of masculine imagery for God. From the standpoint of both-and thinking, God is
both male and female. Even better, God is the negation and affirmation of all gender. Lee is hesitant to speak of an androgynous
deity, because God ultimately transcends all gender (*TC* 50-52). The
pronoun "it" might be better than "he" or "she" for God, although all three are ultimately inadequate. God as change encompasses both the feminine (yin) and masculine (yang) dimensions
of reality (cf. *CR* 95).

THE INADEQUACY OF DIVINE IMPASSIBILITY

One of Lee's main criticisms of the theology of the absolute is
its affirmation of divine impassibility. He does not attempt a sur-

---

[9]Lee ignores the strong theriomorphic tradition in primitive religions
(i.e., describing deity as animals).

vey of the history of this doctrine, but he evaluates its major assumptions and arguments. His main criterion for the evaluation is the loving nature of God. If God is love, as the Bible indicates, he must empathize with the world and suffer with it. Before investigating further his defense of divine suffering, I should examine his critique of divine impassibility, which is one of the fullest in recent literature. In many cases he is more rigorous in his critique than any other figure we have studied.

Focusing on the early history of Christianity, Lee cites three basic assumptions underlying the doctrine of divine impassibility. Like many critics of impassibility, Lee takes Greek philosophy to be the primary villain in the distortion of the faith. First, the development of the doctrine of the Trinity led to an overemphasis on the distinctions among the three persons of the Trinity. The patripassianists were considered heretics because they failed to uphold these distinctions to the satisfaction of the orthodox Christians. In *Adversus Praxean* Tertullian claimed that Praxeas and other patripassianists had "crucified the Father." The patripassianists' basic concern was to protect the unity of God and avoid a tritheism. The result was the implication that God the Father suffered and died with the Son on the cross. Tertullian even argued that the Father was incapable of any compassion or "fellow-suffering" with Christ. The emerging orthodox doctrine of the Trinity insisted that the Son alone suffered and died.

Lee criticizes this first assumption for stressing unduly the trinitarian distinctions. The early church compounded the problem by insisting that when Christ was crucified only the human nature suffered. Overall the church made such a sharp demarcation between Father and Son and between divine and human natures that it neglected their "mutual participation in their experience of suffering" (*GS* 36). The early church was caught in the tension between a tritheistic and a monarchian concept of God. The church chose to move dangerously close to a tritheism in order to keep the Father from suffering. Lee suggests that divine suffering or empathy protects the mutual involvement of all three persons of the Trinity. He concludes that "we reject in light of the empathy of God the validity of both modalistic monarchianism, which asserts the unity without distinctions, and antipatripassianism, which emphasizes the distinction without a genuine unity" (*GS* 37). In addition, Lee rejects the separation of divine and human natures in Christ as artificial. From the standpoint of divine empathy, there is no difficulty in assuming that suffering touches the human as well as the divine dimension of Christ's life.

The second assumption is the Greek idea of divine *apatheia*. Greek philosophers, especially the Stoics, developed the notion that God did not feel any emotion or passion. In general, Greek thought elevated reason above emotions or passions. Human reason enables man to be in tune with the divine reason or *logos*, according to the Stoics. A similar attitude prevailed in Neoplatonism. If feeling or passion is inferior to reason, then man should use his reason to suppress it and achieve *apatheia* or emotionlessness. The ideal of *apatheia* applies to God also. Passion or pathos is not compatible with the dignity of deity. Lee suggests that the basic motive underlying divine apathy is the "dread of anthropomorphism" (*GS* 38). For Lee there is a basic contradiction between affirming God's love and denying he feels. If God does not feel, he is not a God of love. He agrees with the Greeks that as long as passion connotes irrational, capricious moods or feelings, it is not appropriate for God. Passion or pathos as Lee understands it is not irrational or subrational, rather it is transrational. "It is not a blind impulse but a passionate participation to love the unlovable" (*GS* 39).

The third assumption behind divine impassibility is the Greek idea of divine *autarkeia* (*GS* 30-32). Many of the Greek philosophers argued that deity must be perfect, self-sufficient, contented, and unmoved. Plato and Aristotle both concurred that God was ultimately immovable on the basis of *autarkeia* and a static world view. Aristotle's God, for example, was an unmoved mover incapable of change. Later, Thomas Aquinas claimed that God was pure actuality (*actus purus*), also eliminating the possibility of change for God. Lee is most disturbed here by the static world view associated with *autarkeia*. A dynamic ontology, such as he derives from the *I ching*, allows for the interaction of God with the world. God acts in the world and reacts to the world. God changes because of his empathy for the world, but his basic attitude or will for the world is unchanging (*GS* 41).

Having concluded that these three assumptions are invalid because they contradict divine empathy, Lee examines three objections to the doctrine of divine passibility. First, some have objected that suffering is intrinsically evil and thus cannot be part of God's experience. A suffering God would be pitied rather than worshiped. The key issue here is a view of salvation (*GS* 33). If God suffers, can he help the sufferer? If all suffering is evil, a perfectly good God cannot experience it. Lee responds that suffering is not inherently evil. Some suffering is freely chosen and redemptive, other suffering is caused by evil. "The general suffering (or penal suffering) is *effected* by an evil, while the redemptive suffering is *occasioned* by it" (*GS* 42). This general suffering can be evil, but redemptive suffering is intrinsically good and is designed to overcome evil. In addition, Lee notes that the traditional notion of divine bliss is based on a static ontology. The Christian grants that God may experience disturbance, but ultimately the disturbance is overcome.

The second objection is that suffering implies frustration (*GS* 34). Since God has infinite power and freedom, any frustration would imply that God is limited. The self-sufficient God cannot be so limited or frustrated. Divine passibility necessarily implies a finite God. Lee admits that God cannot experience pain such as ours because he is not physical. God can be frustrated, however, in the case of his self-limitation. Self-limitation and empathy are characteristic of God. "In the empathy of God there is a paradoxical union between the self-sufficiency in His essential nature and the self-limitation in His existential situation" (*GS* 44).

The third objection is that suffering entails involvement in the time process. If God is really eternal and transcendent, he cannot be entangled in time. According to Lee, God both created time and participates in it. We need to keep a paradoxical balance, he insists, between "God in time" and "time in God" even though "time in God" has the priority (*GS* 44).

Lee concludes that the doctrine of divine impassibility is based primarily on the assumptions and perspectives of Greek philosophy rather than the biblical witness. His proposal about divine empathy, he argues, is closer to the dynamic ontology of the Bible. In the next section of this chapter I will focus on Lee's alternative.

THE EMPATHY OF GOD

Lee bases his affirmation of divine suffering on God's nature as love (*agape*) and divine empathy. Lee's thesis is that "*Agape* is the basis of divine empathy, while the empathy of God is a mode of *Agape*" (*GS* 13). My goal in this section is to clarify Lee's arguments, especially as they are developed in *God Suffers for Us*.

For Lee, *agape* is the essential content of the Christian faith and the fundamental characteristic of God. Christianity is founded on the claim that "God is love" (1 John 4:8). Lee refuses to consider love as merely an attribute of God, as if something else were more basic to God's nature. It is God's nature to love; loving is not merely one of several qualities of God. God's actions flow from his loving nature. Lee describes *agape* as an outgoing concern for others that transforms the unlovable into the lovable. Lee also rejects the attempt to restrict God's love to the New Testament by suggesting that his holiness is central to the Old Testament. God's holiness and love are mutually dependent and inclusive. "Holiness is the presupposition of love, while love is the fulfillment of holiness" (*GS* 9). In fact, Lee describes holiness as the transcendent character of love.

Divine empathy is a function of God's *agape* nature. Lee is careful to distinguish divine sympathy and empathy. Sympathy is often used as a basis for divine suffering, but Lee demurs: sympathy is an emotional identification, but empathy is an actual participation. Sympathy is basically a reactive feeling, while *agape* is spontaneous. Sympathy tends to be based on preference; we sympathize most easily with those we already like. Sympathy can easily be selfish. *Agape*, on the other hand, is a living participation that creates worth and lovableness in the unlovable. This understanding of empathy correlates with the biblical emphasis on the I-Thou relationship within the Godhead and between man and God. Jesus is one with the Father because of participation rather than imaginary emotional identification. Our relationship with God is a reflection of this prototypical I-Thou paradigm. For Lee, divine empathy is a better conceptualization of God's suffering than divine sympathy. God does not merely feel with (sympathy) the human situation; he feels himself into (empathy) the human situation and actively participates in it.

God's empathy leads to suffering as he experiences an inner tension between his holiness and love. God's love has two dimensions that are dialectically united: the transcendental (holiness and righteousness) and the immanental (grace and mercy). *Agape* is the paradoxical unity of these two dimensions. This relationship is disturbed by sin, and the tension is experienced as the wrath of God. The wrath of God is "a symbol of the struggling love of God to accept that which is also rejected by Him" (*GS* 15). Divine wrath is seen by Lee as a restrained form of God's love entirely compatible with his basic *agape* nature.

Lee further clarifies the distinction between pain and suffering. "Pain is defined in terms of a sensation bound to the body, while suffering is in terms of a loving relationship bound to time" (*GS* 4-5). Pain is restricted to the physical while suffering is much more complex, comprising psychological and spiritual dimensions. Lee recognizes that in human beings pain and suffering are interrelated as, for example, in the case of psychosomatic illness. Because God does not have a body, he does not feel pain. Because the intensity of suffering depends on the intimacy of the relationship, God suffers the most intensely of all. There is, of course, the potential for suffering in any loving relationship. "The intensity of suffering increases in proportion to the intensity of the loving relationship" (*GS* 17-18). Lee notes that God suffers only as a result of human suffering and sin. *Agape* includes the potential for suffering, yet the actualization of suffering requires God's empathy with the world.

Although Lee builds his case primarily on God's *agape* nature, he points to the Servant of the Lord in Deutero-Isaiah as a vivid symbol of divine suffering. He focuses especially on Isaiah 52:13-53:12. The suffering servant suffers deep humiliation. God's suffering, like the servant's, is the greatest possible kind of suffering. "Since the intensity of suffering is proportionate to the intimacy of the relationship, the God who relates Himself unconditionally to love the world is the greatest sufferer of all" (*GS* 21). Again like the servant, God is suffering vicariously and graciously, and suffering on behalf of others rather than for himself. Finally, God's suffering is redemptive. We will see shortly how divine suffering can help alleviate human suffering.

Lee supports his case for divine passibility by considering its compatibility with several major Christian doctrines. He does not intend necessarily to develop a new systematic theology, but he hopes to show that divine passibility is more in keeping with key doctrines than is divine impassibility.[10] First, he focuses on the doctrine of creation, which he insists has been unfortunately neglected by most theologians. He suggests that this doctrine is "the most important affirmation of the Judeo-Christian faith" (*TC* 67). Most theologians have overemphasized salvation and de-emphasized creation, yet creation is the presupposition for redemption. According to Lee, creation is the first externalization of the eternal empathic relationship within the Godhead. The covenant relationship God establishes with the Hebrews is simply an extension of his empathy for the world. Lee agrees with Karl Barth that the creation is the external basis for the covenant, and the covenant is the internal basis for creation (*GS* 48). Divine impassibility is incompatible with creation because it assumes God is indifferent to the world. Divine passibility can affirm the goodness of creation and God's continuing concern for it much more readily than divine impassibility. Evil and suffering within the world form the occasion for God's suffering. His willingness to create the world points to his willingness to care for it.

Second, Lee turns to the Incarnation as the "most perfect form of divine empathy" (*GS* 52). The significance of the Incarnation transcends its value as a historical event. The Incarnation was not so much a transformation of the divine into the human as a participation of God in human life. The Incarnation is the fullest realization of the empathy that always characterizes God's nature. Divine impassibility cannot comprehend the Incarnation because of its artificial, sharp differentiation between the divine and human natures. "To deny the unity of experience between human and divine in Christ is in a way to deny the reality of incarnation" (*GS*

---

[10]In *CR*, *TC*, and *GS*, however, Lee has treated almost every topic in systematic theology from his perspective.

54). The Incarnation was the revelation of *agape* and the perfect realization of God's empathy for mankind. The Incarnation, when
seen from the standpoint of divine passibility, is not an exception
to God's character but rather the supreme historical actualization
and basis for divine passibility.[11] Divine suffering did not begin or
end in the Incarnation; it was intensified there.

Third, Lee discusses the atonement and pictures the cross as
"the depth of divine empathy" (*GS* 58). The cross epitomizes God's
loving, reconciling action in Christ. The cross was not, however, a
solitary event in human history. "It is the eternal cross in the heart
of God" that is revealed in the cross of Jesus (*GS* 58). The cross is
ultimately an inner act of God that was externalized on Calvary;
"the eternal cross is the prototype of the historic cross" (*GS* 59). The
agony of Christ on the cross points to the empathy and suffering
of God. Lee realizes the danger of pushing his position toward a
death-of-God theology. One can speak of God suffering and dying
only in the context of the resurrection. Lee further argues that God's
love cannot be redemptive without suffering. "To deny the suffering of God is to deny the redemptive work of God" (*GS* 60). If only
the human nature of Christ suffered, then the cross has no saving
efficacy. For Lee, divine passibility is a necessary correlate of the
atonement. In terms of historic atonement theories, Lee feels most
comfortable with the classic theory articulated by Gustaf Aulen because it emphasizes that the atonement is God's work from beginning to end. God suffers intensely in Christ and in his own right
as suffering continues in the world.

Fourth, Lee describes the Holy Spirit as the active presence of
God in the world. Divine empathy is an activity of God's spirit. As
we saw earlier, Lee refuses to allow trinitarian distinctions to become so rigid that tritheism results. If empathy characterizes the
Father in creation and the Son in redemption, then it must also
mark the Holy Spirit. Empathy characterizes the Spirit's relation
with the rest of the Godhead as well as with mankind. Christian
koinonia (community, fellowship) is based on Christians partici-

---

[11]In Lee's later writings he is less willing to stress the uniqueness of
Christ; cf. *CR* 48, *TC* 88.

pating in the Holy Spirit. "*Koinonia* is, then, the community of human participation in the Holy Spirit who becomes the subject of all those who participate in the community" (*GS* 65). The activity of the Holy Spirit is incompatible with divine impassibility. An immutable, inactive God cannot be empathic. Thus Lee understands the Holy Spirit to be the continuing manifestation of divine passibility.

Fifth, Lee sees the Trinity as an archetype of divine empathy. The *agape* that characterizes the relations among Father, Son, and Holy Spirit is revealed historically in the empathy God has for mankind. The revelation of God in the world mirrors the empathic relations of the Trinity. Lee believes this view avoids the classic heresies of subordinationism and modalism. In other words, no member of the Trinity is subordinate to the others, and the members of the Trinity do not lose their distinctive identities (*GS* 73).[12] In this context Lee is also careful to note that God does not suffer simply as a response to human suffering. The possibility of divine suffering is intrinsic to God's eternal nature.

> God's suffering is not something which comes from His response to human sufferings, but He has been involved in His own suffering even much before the tragedy of man in history. The significance of the inner-trinitarian life of God as the prototype of divine empathy lies in this, that all the experiences of tragedy and suffering between God and man in the world must be anticipated in the inner community of Father, Son, and the Holy Spirit (*GS* 75).

Christ's suffering on the cross was a revelation of the suffering of the Father and Holy Spirit as well. Lee does not identify himself as a patripassianist because he does allow for distinctions among the three persons of the Trinity, yet he criticizes the antipatripassianist for making these distinctions too rigid. He uses Paul's analogy of the body of Christ to illustrate the suffering of the entire Trinity. In the inner divine community of the Trinity, the suffering of any member implies the suffering of all three equally.

-----

[12]In *TC* 113 Lee describes the Trinity as change (Father), yang (Son), and yin (Spirit).

In general, Lee concludes that divine empathy and passibility are viable interpretations of the Christian faith. Divine empathy is a valid expression of God's *agape* nature, and divine passibility is compatible with the major doctrines of the Christian faith. In fact, Lee believes he has demonstrated that divine impassibility is contradictory to these same doctrines.

Lee also tries to demonstrate that divine passibility helps overcome human suffering. His thesis is that God overcomes our suffering through his suffering. God does not eliminate the reality of human suffering, but he helps people to bear their suffering in the right way. Lee proposes that there is a fellowship of divine and human suffering. God participates in human suffering even before we know of it. Lee grants that the Bible never offers a rational, theoretical theodicy that explains why people suffer, but it does call for trust in God. He suggests that "faith emancipates us from suffering *alone* to be suffering *with*" (*GS* 81). This faith response brings about a "transformation of meaning" that entails a recognition of the meaningfulness of suffering. Our suffering can become voluntary, vicarious, and redemptive rather than involuntary, penal, and general. The concrete expression of the fellowship of divine and human suffering is the church.

The fellowship of suffering between God and man produces three factors that help overcome suffering. First, this fellowship gives "the *meaning* of positive significance to our suffering" (*GS* 84). Our suffering becomes meaningful rather than meaningless. All suffering is also God's suffering. Suffering that has meaning can be endured. Second, the fellowship of suffering offers strength to endure our suffering. Suffering can create an obstacle between God and man, but God's love is a source of strength to us. Third, the fellowship of suffering gives us hope to anticipate the joy of eternal life. Here Lee introduces the eschatological dimension of his theodicy. He does not divorce the present from the future, for the joy of the future is latent in the present. He does note, however, that a fuller joy awaits the final consummation of time. The Christian cannot escape all suffering in this finite existence, but the redeemed do have their suffering "lifted to a new level" (*GS* 88). Suffering continues but is understood in light of the resources of divine love and empathy.

ANALOGY, ANTHROPOPATHISM, AND AMBIGUITY

Lee's doctrine of God, especially his emphasis on divine suffering, is one of the most stimulating we have seen. Especially salutary is his derivation of divine suffering from God's *agape* nature. As he argues, "Love and suffering are in an inseparable unity. If the divine love is greater than the human love, divine suffering must be greater than human suffering. To deny the possibility of divine suffering is to deny the possibility of divine love altogether" (*CR* 76). Lee works out the systematic implications of divine empathy more carefully than most other proponents of divine suffering. Although several aspects of his thought merit further consideration and critique, I will isolate only one major issue. This concern involves a possible shift in Lee's position away from a more biblical emphasis on divine *agape* toward a more monistic, mystical view of God. In *God Suffers for Us*, Lee's primary support for divine empathy and passibility was God's loving nature.[13] In other writings Lee has produced a theology more strongly influenced by the *I ching* and an apparently monistic view of reality. This shift is evident in several aspects of his thought, but here I will focus only on the reach and limits of analogical language about God. In general, Lee seems to be moving away from the way of analogy, which permits the use of anthropopathic descriptions of God with some caution, and toward the mystical way of negation, which denies the appropriateness of these anthropopathisms.

In his earlier work, *God Suffers for Us*, Lee is sympathetic to Karl Barth's view of the analogy of faith (or analogy of relation).[14] Barth and Lee modify the traditional way of analogy. These analogy descriptions of God are seen as such based on partial correspondences between God and finite reality. Because God is transcendent, human language can never correspond exactly to

---

[13]*GS* is based on Lee's dissertation in 1968. Almost all of his later writings use the *I ching* more prominently.

[14]*GS* 91-103 is based on "Karl Barth's Use of Analogy in His Church Dogmatics," *Scottish Journal of Theology* 22 (June 1969): 129-51.

God, but these analogies were partially adequate and avoided two extremes—univocity and equivocity (*GS* 4). Univocity assumed a term could apply to God and finite objects equally well, thereby rejecting divine transcendence. Equivocity assumed a term could not apply to God and finite objects with the same meaning, thereby neglecting divine immanence. The way of analogy tried to avoid these extremes and allow for the use of human categories for God. Lee agreed that the analogy of faith was a better theological method (cf. Romans 12:6). Human knowledge of God is imperfect, but in faith one can speak meaningfully of God. Lee especially emphasized the value of the language of interpersonal relations in describing God. The analogy of faith is an analogy of relation. Lee agrees with Barth that analogical language should not be tied to the medieval analogy of being, which assumed an unbroken continuity of nature between God, man, and the finite world. The analogy of being jeopardized the transcendence of God. Personalistic language has limitations, but since the Bible emphasizes it, it should be basic to our theology. The analogy of faith is much better than the analogy of being for understanding divine passibility because it allows for personal, christological, dynamic categories (*GS* 100-103). In this earlier work, then, Lee was willing to develop his view of divine suffering from the anthropomorphic and anthropopathic descriptions of God in the Bible (e.g., love, wrath). He recognizes the danger that these descriptions may make God appear too much like man, even as they do maintain the personal, dynamic character of God.

As noted, Lee has lately allowed his use of the *I ching* to push him toward a more monistic, mystical understanding of God.[15] In *The Theology of Change*, for example, Lee stresses the nonsymbolic nature of God and de-emphasizes the value of personalistic descriptions of God. He depicts the name Yahweh as so mystical and mysterious that God is basically nameless and incomprehensible to man (*TC* 31-32; *CR* 16). When he describes God in this later work,

---

[15]See, for example, the several references to Meister Eckhart in *TC*. Lee is apparently sympathetic to the Eckhart proposal of a Godhead that transcends God as we know him.

he focuses on impersonal categories and stresses the inadequacy of personalistic concepts. Many Christians no doubt would grant that some impersonal categories are appropriate to God (e.g., rock). My concern is that Lee's later thought may be governed too much by the *I ching's* metaphysic rather than the biblical revelation. Anyone who proposes a new understanding of the Christian faith in light of a different world view expects this type of criticism. Lee is not wrong to try an Eastern interpretation of the Christian faith. The problem is in allowing the Eastern view to distort the biblical witness. Lee attempts to uphold the integrity of the Christian faith and the Eastern mentality, but on this issue he seems to sacrifice the former for the latter. His earlier stress on divine love, empathy, and passibility is jeopardized by the *I ching*. At the least, there is now a basic ambiguity in Lee's position.

In *The Theology of Change* Lee's movement toward monism is evident, for example, in his discussion of God's relationship to evil. Following the both-and way of thinking, Lee insists that God must somehow encompass good and evil. If God does not include evil, a dualism would result. He argues that the earliest traditions of the Old Testament were monistic, but a "foreign dualism" later came about as the result of Babylonian and Persian influence. The New Testament unfortunately preserves the dualistic world view.[16] Most Christian theologians have tried to steer a middle course between monism and dualism, but Lee seems to lean heavily toward the monistic interpretation of the faith. According to John Hick, Christian monotheism must avoid two poles, dualism and monism.[17] Monism, he suggests, does not recognize that evil is truly evil and opposed to God's will. Dualism errs by absolutizing the opposition between good and evil. Hick proposes that the Christian faith is best seen as a "present dualism within the ultimate setting of an

---

[16]Cf. Lee, "Bultmann's Existentialist Interpretation and the Problem of Evil," *Journal of Religious Thought* 26 (Autumn-Winter 1969): 65-80; "Interpreting the Demonic Powers in Pauline Thought," *Novum Testamentum* 12 (January 1970): 54-69.

[17]See John Hick, *Evil and the God of Love* (London: Collins, 1968) 21-39.

unqualifiedly monotheistic faith."[18] Lee follows his both-and way of thought so rigorously that he must elevate God above the good-evil distinction. God includes both good and evil in his nature, yet the good-evil distinction is really only appropriate for those in finite existence. "Evil is existential, not essential, because it became real in humanity's transition from essence to existence" (*TC* 59).[19] Because God transcends all finite categories, the good-evil distinction is not ultimately valid for him. Lee further argues that good and evil are mutually interdependent and inclusive. Good-evil is a phenomenal distinction that is ultimately illusory and relative (*TC* 60).

Lee does not pursue this line of argument to its logical conclusion, which would be pantheism or monism. He suggests that God "transcends the distinction between good and evil but is a part of the struggle between them" (*TC* 61). The implication throughout his discussion, however, is that the problem of suffering is a human problem rather than a divine one. Thus "the problem of evil lies not with the nature of God but with our way of thinking" (*TC* 57). One wonders in what sense Lee can affirm divine passibility now. He still proposes the category, but now it is a consequence of the yin-yang relationship. Christ's suffering is also the Father's suffering, but one is not sure if the Father really suffers now. Even the yin-yang scheme is superseded by change as the ultimate reality. Christ's suffering is real, but in the theology of change evil is always counterbalanced by some good.

In his later thought, Lee also questions the necessity of God's overcoming evil. He argues that discussion of eliminating evil reflects a dualistic world view inappropriate to the Christian faith. "Thus elimination is not a valid solution to the problem of evil. God deals with the problem of evil by enabling reversion from it to its polar opposite—good" (*TC* 61). Lee insists that Jesus understood evil in its complementary relationship with good even though the cosmic dualism of that time obscured his message.

---

[18]Ibid., 22.

[19]Here, as in many other places, Lee is using a distinction derived from existentialist thought, especially Bultmann and Tillich.

The basic ambiguity in Lee's later thought can be seen in light of his theodicy and our central question: Does God suffer? Is the tragedy or sorrow of the world real for God, or is Lee proposing an eternal, undisturbed divine bliss? In his early work Lee keeps the suffering of God a permanent dimension of God's experience. He suggests that "eternal bliss is not the absence of divine suffering but the victory of His suffering over the evil of the world" (*GS* 43). In his later work Lee no longer stresses divine empathy in the context of the analogy of faith. Instead, any anthropopathic language is dismissed in favor of a God who cannot be comprehended by human analogy. He still refers in passing to God's suffering, but the main emphasis is on God's transcendence of categories such as passible and impassible, male and female, good and evil, and personal and impersonal. The yin-yang system is "based on essential monism and existential dualism" (*TC* 117). My question is whether or not an ultimately monistic theology can allow for divine passibility. Indeed, one wonders if perhaps the "divine aesthete" charge raised against process theology by Stephen Ely might not be more appropriately directed at Lee's theology of change. When Lee worked within the context of the analogy of faith, he seemed better able to cope with the biblical anthropopathisms than he can now in the fully developed theology of change. Although Lee now insists that God is change itself, receptive to the world, one wonders if his monism does not ultimately lead to an undisturbed deity. For example, Lee suggests that good and evil are like waves in the ocean: "The waves move, but they are a surface phenomenon; they do not affect the water below" (*TC* 60). If God as change itself totally transcends good and evil and all finite categories, perhaps even divine empathy or *agape* is no longer appropriate. In any event, Lee needs to clarify the relationship of *God Suffers for Us* to the later works based on the *I ching*.

One further reservation about Lee's theodicy deserves attention. In all of his work Lee tends to stress the passive nature of man's response to suffering. In *God Suffers for Us* he develops the concept of the fellowship of divine and human suffering. Our suffering is overcome by our participation in God's suffering. Basically, it seems human suffering is alleviated by the knowledge of divine suffering and the hope of a future relief. He emphasizes the endurance of suffering and the way in which suffering reminds us of our finitude.

> Through our endurance in suffering we come to learn that we are limited and we cannot control our own destiny. We learn from suffering that it is not we but God who rules the world. When we learn obedience from what we suffered, our false pride which alienates us from God is transformed into real humanity through humiliation (*GS* 88-89).

In later works Lee again stresses the passive nature of man's response to his predicament. Any kind of action or self-assertion is contrary to the theology of change. "Activism is the enemy of Change. The changes which man initiates are the countermovements of the Change. The best way for him to behave is to be totally receptive to the change" (*CR* 39; cf. *TC* 94-95).[20] Although some stress on humility and passivity is appropriate to a discussion of salvation by divine initiative, the danger is that Lee will neglect the need for human action to alleviate suffering. It appears that in Lee's system human beings have no incentive or reason to initiate programs or institutions to limit human suffering. Like Kitamori, Lee relies too much on a mystical, soteriological resolution to the problem of suffering. Christians have a stronger empathy for the suffering of others due to their recognition of divine empathy and should provide a fellowship for the suffering. They do not, it seems, work politically or in any other way to counteract suffering. God suffers with us, but does he encourage us to work against suffering?

In conclusion, Lee's effort to describe the suffering of God is one of the most thorough and successful in recent decades. His attempt to do Christian theology in the context of Eastern thought is commendable. His adaptation of the *I ching*, though, may have created some ambiguity about his understanding of divine suffer-

---

[20]In his later work Lee stresses that salvation comes through knowledge and perhaps leaves himself open to the charge of gnosticism. See *CR* 37-38.

ing. Still, his basic affirmation is generally correct: "The concept of divine suffering is not only the core of our faith but the uniqueness of Christianity" (*GS* 1).

Chapter Eight

The Wounded Healer

While discussing the task of ministry in a suffering world, Henri Nouwen retells a Jewish legend preserved in the Talmud about the Messiah as a wounded healer. A Jewish rabbi asked Elijah the prophet when the Messiah would appear. Elijah responded that the rabbi could ask the Messiah himself. "How shall I know him?" asked the rabbi. "He is sitting among the poor covered with wounds. The others unbind all their wounds at the same time and then bind them up again. But he unbinds one at a time and binds it up again, saying to himself, 'Perhaps I shall be needed: if so I must always be ready so as not to delay for a moment.' "[1] If the actions of the Messiah can be taken as a clue to the nature of God, then God too is a wounded healer. God is the *wounded* healer because he experiences the pain and agony of the world. He is the wounded *healer* because his suffering is essential to his efforts to heal the world's wounds. The six theologians discussed here would agree that God suffers as part of his redemptive activity in human history.

In examining these six theologians, I have noted some possible criticisms. At this point I will not attempt a fuller critique of each one. Instead, my goal in this chapter is to raise two questions that need further attention. First, what is the relation of God's passion to his providence? Second, what is the relation of God's passion to human attempts at alleviating suffering? At the outset we saw that

---

[1]Henri J. M. Nouwen, *The Wounded Healer: Ministry in Contemporary Society* (Garden City NY: Doubleday, 1972) 83-84.

many Christians are perplexed by the theodicy issue. Why do we
suffer? Why does God allow or cause suffering? All six theologians
would agree that their viewpoints are not intended to be idle, theoretical speculation. Each saw the passion of God as having a direct bearing on human suffering. In this chapter, then, I will raise
the "so what" question. If God suffers, what difference does that
make to human suffering? As these questions are answered from
the divine-passibility perspective, that perspective will become
even more cogent.

PROVIDENCE AND THE PASSION OF GOD

What effect does divine suffering have on human suffering?
Basically proponents of divine suffering affirm God's companionship with us in our suffering. God is not detached and aloof from
human anguish; he is intensely aware of our agony and responds
to it. Moltmann's crucified God suffers with us now and promises
an eschatological resolution to suffering. Cone's God of the oppressed identifies with the blackness of the human situation.
MacGregor's kenotic God is in touch with human misery although
he does not interfere in human affairs. Kitamori proposes a mysticism of the pain of God in which human suffering is overcome.
Daniel Day Williams's dipolar God is sensitive to our predicament
and lures all of reality toward a more peaceful condition. Jung Lee's
God empathizes with mankind and offers a fellowship of divine
and human suffering. In general, all would concur that human
suffering is made bearable because of the divine passion.

Each could use the biblical image of God as the wounded healer.
God heals the wounds of the world through his own wounds. God
is not helpless in the world; rather, his healing strength is exem-
plified in his suffering. "His power reaches its apex in the compassionate love that takes to itself the agony and tragedy of the
world and thereby heals and transforms it."[2] This theme is clear in
both testaments. Describing the suffering servant of Yahweh,

---

[2]S. Paul Schilling, *God and Human Anguish* (Nashville: Abingdon, 1977)
258.

Deutero-Isaiah notes that "with his stripes we are healed" (53:5). Pointing to the crucifixion of Christ, Peter agrees that "by his wounds you have been healed" (1 Peter 2:24). Or, as Bonhoeffer so graphically put it: "God lets himself be pushed out of the world on to the cross. He is weak and powerless in the world, and that is precisely the way, the only way in which he is with us and helps us."[3]

Although these six theologians try to relate God's suffering to human suffering, most fail to develop an adequate overall view of divine providence. Indeed, they would generally provide further support for the claim that the doctrine of providence is "the forgotten stepchild of contemporary theology."[4] To be more specific, most of the six neglect several key issues that are essential to a full-fledged view of providence. A more comprehensive response to human suffering by these six will require additional attention to other facets of divine providence. Two issues in particular have been neglected by these six: the origin of suffering and the distribution of suffering. First, what is the origin of suffering? This issue has long perplexed Christians, but several of our six theologians have not wrestled with it directly. Most would apparently agree with Moltmann's claim that for the twentieth century moral evil rather than natural evil is the primary concern.[5] People are most disturbed about man's inhumanity to man (moral evil) than about "natural" calamities such as tornadoes and cancer. As a consequence, these theologians have neglected the traditional question of suffering's origin. The cause of moral evil is man; the cause of natural evil is not discussed. They have focused on God's suffering with mankind but have not asked about God's responsibility for the genesis of suffering. Even if God's suffering with us enables us to bear our suffering now, why did he allow/cause it in the

---

[3]Dietrich Bonhoeffer, *Letters and Papers from Prison*, rev. ed., ed. Eberhard Bethge (New York: Macmillan, 1967) 188.

[4]Langdon B. Gilkey, "The Concept of Providence in Contemporary Theology," *Journal of Religion* 43 (July 1963): 174.

[5]Jürgen Moltmann, *Religion, Revolution, and the Future*, trans. M. Douglas Meeks (New York: Charles Scribner's Sons, 1969) 205.

first place? Some of the six theologians would likely reply that such a question is unanswerable. James Cone, for example, argues that the "weight of the Biblical view of suffering is not on the *origin* of evil but on what God in Christ has done about evil."[6] Cone's non-speculative, confessional approach to this issue is typical of all six. Only MacGregor and Williams really sketch a theology sweeping enough to respond to this question.

Undoubtedly no one explanation of the origin of suffering is necessitated by the doctrine of divine passibility. Belief in divine passion, as we have seen, can arise from a variety of contexts. Perhaps a number of theories about the origin of evil and suffering could be compatible with the passion of God. It is likely, however, that a view emphasizing divine love and human freedom would be most cogent. All six theologians have used God's love as a basis for his suffering. Likewise God suffers to a great degree because of human failure to respond to his love.[7] If these themes are carried over to the question of the origin of suffering, then God is not directly responsible for human suffering. Much, perhaps most, human suffering is due to human action.[8] Perhaps this awareness prompted the contemporary preoccupation with moral evil rather than natural evil. These six figures have apparently assumed God is only indirectly responsible for human suffering. The direct responsibility is generally human. God created a world with the possibility of suffering, but he is not accused of causing suffering per se. Quite likely most of these six would agree that much human suffering is due to the misuse of human freedom. A loving God created a world marked by finite freedom and the possibility of its misuse. When the possibility of suffering is actualized, God responds out of his suffering love.

This brief sketch of a theory for the origin of suffering is only one possibility within the context of divine suffering. Process the-

---

[6]James Cone, *God of the Oppressed* (New York: Seabury Press, 1975) 174.

[7]Jung Young Lee, *God Suffers for Us: A Systematic Inquiry into a Concept of Divine Passibility* (The Hague: Martinus Nijhoff, 1974) 16.

[8]C. S. Lewis, *The Problem of Pain* (New York: Macmillan, 1962) 89, suggests that four-fifths of human suffering may be due to human agency.

ology probably comes the closest to articulating a clear position here. Yet overall, contemporary proponents of divine passion have given adequate attention to the presence of God in the midst of suffering while overlooking the origin of suffering. They generally also point to the final, eschatological elimination of suffering as part of their theodicy. They have not, however, focused sufficiently on the origin of suffering. Such a move would help them produce a comprehensive doctrine of providence.

Second, many people are more concerned about the distribution of suffering than about the mere fact of suffering.[9] Given that suffering is an almost inevitable ingredient in human existence, sufferers often ask why they suffer more than others. James Cone, for example, uses divine suffering to respond to the charge that God is a white racist who brings extra suffering to blacks.[10] Many of the biblical laments reflect this concern about the distribution of suffering more than the speculative concern about the origin of suffering. If some suffering is expected, why do some suffer more than others? Here all Christian theologians are caught in a real dilemma, since it seems that God's love and power are incompatible. Proponents of divine suffering have generally highlighted God's love, and some have redefined divine power in light of that love. MacGregor probably represents the extreme position here with his view of divine power. He argues that because God loves the world, he does not exercise power in it. His kenotic love necessitates the abdication of power as it is traditionally conceived. Williams's process perspective calls for understanding power as persuasion instead of coercion. In terms of the traditional theodicy issue, proponents of divine passion generally take divine *agape* as the criterion for defining divine power. They have failed, however, to apply this criterion adequately to the problem of the distribution of suffering. If God's love is normative, why does he allow suffering to occur so unevenly? Here again no one uniform response is required of all adherents of divine passion. One possible response

---

[9]Cone, *God of the Oppressed*, 165.

[10]For the charge, see William R. Jones, *Is God a White Racist? A Preamble to Black Theology* (Garden City NY: Doubleday, 1973).

would again be to rely on the misuse of human freedom as a major explanatory factor. Some suffer more than others because one group or individual exercises its finite freedom in a demonic fashion. Hence in the case of a Hitler, God should not be blamed for the slaughter of six million Jews by the Germans. God created a world in which Hitler was a possibility, but God did not create Hitler or the Holocaust. To ask God to intervene in such situations unilaterally would jeopardize the human freedom that is used responsibly in many other situations. To more fully develop this type of argument, one could hold to divine passion while acknowledging the inequity of human suffering.

A difficulty common to both questions is that the proponents of divine passion do not take into account all forms of suffering. In both cases, appeal to the misuse of human freedom may alleviate the problem of divine responsibility: God does not directly cause suffering per se, and he does not directly plan the distribution of suffering. This response still does not take into account the origin and distribution of so-called natural evil. Even if men acted humanely and responsibly at all times, presumably suffering would still be caused by tornadoes, leukemia, and other natural disasters. Certainly God suffers with the leukemia victim and did as well with the Holocaust victim in World War II. The question that these six have generally ignored is whether or not God causes natural evil. If human agency is not involved, then God seems a logical choice as the originator of this suffering. Process theologians could still use the misuse-of-freedom argument because for them all of reality possesses some freedom. Any finite reality might refuse to follow God's persuasive power and create the possibility of leukemia or tornadoes. Williams referred in passing to "a mystery of evil in the creation," but he did not clarify how that evil originated. Jung Lee might respond that because of the yin-yang principle and the organic interdependence of all reality, a misuse of human freedom would be ultimately responsible for natural evil. Man's dominion and exploitation of nature has produced multiple forms of pollution. Perhaps misused human freedom could ultimately explain all forms of suffering. In general, however, the passion-of-God position will be taken more seriously when the origin of natural evil, as well as moral evil, and the distribution of evil are dealt with more carefully.

THE WOUNDED HEALERS

Contemporary adherents of divine passion agree that God's suffering alleviates human suffering. God is the wounded *healer*. His suffering is not forced upon him by forces or situations totally beyond his control. Rather, he lovingly responds to human rebellion, pain, and sorrow with a genuine passion. As Jung Lee noted, there is a fellowship of human and divine suffering that encourages and supports the human sufferer.[11] One issue the proponents of divine passion have not yet developed with complete adequacy is the relation of God's passion to human action in alleviating human suffering. Does divine passion function solely as a comfort to sufferers, or does it encourage the sufferer to resist his suffering?

Here the two theologians with an Eastern background offer the least support. Lee and Kitamori both highlight the comforting role of God's passion but neglect the ethical dimension of their position. Lee simply does not treat the issue at any length. He sees activity as incompatible with the theology of change and seems to be comfortable with a mystical tradition that encourages passivity and quietism. Kitamori, on the other hand, treats the ethical dimension of the pain of God and encourages Christians to love the unlovable as part of their service to God's pain. Kitamori does not, however, specify an ethical program in any detail, and a mysticism of pain seems to dominate his position. In fact, Kitamori encourages the Christian to seek out painful situations, and so he leaves himself open to the charge of masochism.[12]

The passion-of-God position *is* compatible with a strong emphasis on human resistance to suffering. Heschel suggested, for

---

[11]Lee, *God Suffers for Us*, 80-90; cf. H. Wheeler Robinson, *Suffering, Human and Divine* (New York: Macmillan, 1939) 185-200.

[12]See Dorothee Soelle, *Suffering*, trans. Everett R. Kalin (Philadelphia: Fortress Press, 1975) 9-32, for a good discussion of Christian masochism and theological sadism.

example, that the Hebrew prophet was a *homo sympathetikos* because of his awareness of God's pathos.[13] The prophet announces
the pathos of God to the people in order to persuade them to re-
pent of their sins, which have occasioned God's pathos. Heschel
contrasts this with the *homo apathetikos* ideal in Stoic philosophy.
For the Stoics the ideal condition of God and man was *apatheia* or
emotionlessness. The passions were to be suppressed. The
prophet, by contrast, was passionate in his concern for the destiny
of the Hebrews and could not be rational or apathetic about their
predicament.

Moltmann agrees with Heschel's position, but universalizes this
sympathetic-man ideal to include the entire Christian life-style. He
suggests that theology and anthropology are reciprocally related.
"Therefore the theology of the 'crucified God' also leads to a cor-
responding anthropology."[14] According to Moltmann, the Christian should be sensitive to the suffering of the world and actively
oppose it. He encourages the Christian to "develop his life in the
field force of the passion of the crucified God."[15] The Christian
should be concerned with the psychological and political liberation of mankind. Awareness of the passion of God, for example,
should produce a political hermeneutics of the Gospel.[16]

James Cone agrees with Moltmann's emphasis on the resistance to human suffering rooted in the passion of God. Cone recognizes that although Christ decisively defeated the forces of evil,
suffering continues until the eschaton. "In the meantime, Christians are called to suffer with God in the fight against evil in the
present age. . . . The oppressed are called to fight against suffering
by becoming God's suffering servants in the world."[17] Cone is es-

---

[13]Abraham J. Heschel, *The Prophets*, vol. 2 (New York: Harper & Row,
1962) 88.

[14]Jürgen Moltmann, *The Crucified God*, trans. R. A. Wilson and John
Bowden (New York: Harper & Row, 1974) 267; cf. Soelle, *Suffering*, 33-59.

[15]Moltmann, *The Crucified God*, 291.

[16]Moltmann, *Religion, Revolution, and the Future*, 83-107.

[17]Cone, *God of the Oppressed*, 177.

pecially critical of the passivity frequently engendered by other-worldly, futuristic interpretations of the Christian faith. Taking the Exodus liberation as his model, Cone argues for liberation of the oppressed by divine and human action. He opposes attempts to alleviate black misery by political activity alone.[18] He emphasizes political activity as a way of participating in God's liberation of blacks. Although such political activity may temporally evoke more suffering, "suffering that arises in the context of the struggle for freedom is liberating. . . . Black people, therefore, as God's Suffering Servant, are called to suffer with and for God in the liberation of humanity."[19]

Daniel Day Williams also sees the passion of God as a stimulus for Christian activity in the present. He opposes any naive, utopian optimism about the future as well as any naive pessimism. The life of Jesus released a power that supports Christians as they work to improve the world.[20] The Christian's love is not primarily an affection but rather an action.[21] Williams emphasizes that God's love, as it is experienced by Christians, should be the foundation of social justice. "The spirit of love requires participation in the 'dirty work' of history."[22] Indeed, love may evoke a protest against injustice, although Williams clearly favors the strategy of nonviolence.

Geddes MacGregor does not develop an ethical system based on the kenotic God, but he does present kenosis as a model for human conduct paralleling God's behavior. "Self-emptying, the principle of the kenotic Being of God, is the law of life."[23] Chris-

---

[18]Ibid., 187-88.

[19]Ibid., 193.

[20]Daniel Day Williams, *God's Grace and Man's Hope* (New York: Harper & Brothers, 1949) 129-35.

[21]Ibid., 148-49.

[22]Daniel Day Williams, *The Spirit and the Forms of Love* (New York: Harper & Row, 1968) 255.

[23]Geddes MacGregor, *He Who Lets Us Be: A Theology of Love* (New York: Seabury Press, 1975) 183.

tians are to be self-emptying and self-abnegating rather than aggressive and self-aggrandizing. Because the greatest good for human beings is sheer existence, Christians have duties rather than rights.[24] The Christian should not expect God to solve his problems magically or supernaturally. Instead, the Christian acts on behalf of the kenotic God to help solve these problems

In general, the passion of God can serve as the basis and resource for human action to oppose suffering. "The awareness that God is involved in the struggle against evil to the point of suffering moves concerned human beings to strive with him."[25] The wounded healer, God suffering in and with mankind, should be joined by a band of wounded healers. Such an emphasis on human activity should not jeopardize God's initiative in history and does not necessitate a humanistic reading of the Christian faith. Rather, Christians should oppose human suffering *because of* God's suffering in the world. A passionate God calls forth passionate people who join him in his struggle against suffering. The wounded healer welcomes wounded healers.

THE COMPASSIONATE GOD

This critical review of contemporary Protestant theologians who affirm divine suffering has highlighted an important issue. Although my purpose in this section is not to develop a full-blown constructive theology of divine suffering, perhaps a few suggestions will point the way to further reflection on this issue. The issue I have raised in this book might seem highly esoteric to some readers, but it actually compels us to reconsider the possibility of a doctrine of God. There are many reasons for contemporary disbelief in God in the late twentieth century, but two seem especially prominent: secularism and suffering.[26] To oversimplify,

---

[24]Ibid., 157.

[25]Schilling, *God and Human Anguish*, 259.

[26]Peter C. Hodgson, *Jesus—Word and Presence: An Essay in Christology* (Philadelphia: Fortress Press, 1971) 2-4, focuses on these two reasons as the context for the contemporary experience of the absence of God.

secularism reaches most of us on an intellectual level while suffering affects us on a more personal and existential level. Indeed, the theodicy issue was the main point of entry for many of us into serious theological reflection. The popularity of books such as Harold Kushner's *When Bad Things Happen to Good People* is a clue to the perennial vitality of this topic.[27] I have already indicated that one serious weakness of many adherents of divine suffering is that they have not developed an overall theodicy. Their emphasis on the passion of God is salutary indeed, but most sufferers desire more than the assurance that God suffers with them. Thoughtful Christians will want to see how divine passion corresponds to other aspects of God's relation to the world. Here I would like to draw together some of the insights reviewed in this volume that will serve as signposts for a fuller theology of divine passion. Openness to the divine-passion concept may not be a panacea for all that ails contemporary theology, but it may lead to a serious reconsideration of the nature of God.

First, a theology of divine suffering needs to be distinctively biblical. All of the theologians considered here have drawn from the biblical witness on the nature of God. Unfortunately, most have not sufficiently shown us the exegetical foundation that supports their conclusion that God suffers. I do not mean to suggest that a Christian understanding of God will ignore the resources of reason, experience, culture, and history, but a distinctively Christian view of God needs a solid exegetical base. Moltmann's critique of a simplistic monotheism and his avowal of an explicitly christocentric, trinitarian view of God are clearly steps in the right direction. MacGregor's recovery of a theology of love and reemphasis on kenosis are also helpful moves. The recent publication of a book on the suffering of God in the Old Testament may signal a renewed interest in this topic in the realm of academic biblical scholarship.[28]

---

[27]Harold S. Kushner, *When Bad Things Happen to Good People* (New York: Avon, 1983). Kushner, a Jew, mentions the suffering of God, attributing it to Christianity (85). Overall, Kushner's theodicy seems closest to MacGregor's view.

[28]Terence E. Fretheim, *The Suffering of God: An Old Testament Perspective* (Philadelphia: Fortress Press, 1984).

Although the biblical writers use a multitude of attributes to explore the mystery of God, perhaps Paul's description of God in 2 Corinthians 1:3 will serve as a clue to guide our thinking: "Praise be to the God and Father of our Lord Jesus Christ, the Father of compassion and the God of all comfort" (NIV). Here Paul focuses on two key attributes: compassion and comfort. To oversimplify, Paul is pointing to God's identity with the human predicament (compassion) and his involvement in responding to that predicament (comfort). The biblical term *compassion* comes closest to the theme of this book, divine suffering.[29] In both testaments God is characterized as a compassionate, sympathetic being who is intimately aware of human suffering. Although many who live in a culture dominated by secularism may never raise the question of God's existence, some struggle explicitly with the character of God. John A. T. Robinson once reflected the popular attitude that God was "morally intolerable" to contemporary people and hence unnecessary.[30] He also cites contemporary novels such as Albert Camus' *The Plague* and Peter DeVries' *The Blood of the Lamb* as reflecting the concerns of many with the character of God. The etymology of the term *theodicy* basically focuses on this concern with God's character: Is God (*theos*) just (*dike*)? As MacGregor and others have aptly said, Christians have often stressed the power of God to the neglect of his goodness. Many today have a nominal belief in God and basically operate from a deistic stance: if there is a God, he really does not care about us. The Yahweh of the Hebrews, however, insisted "I am compassionate" (Exodus 22:27b NIV).

A distinctively Christian view of a suffering God would not ignore the complex issue of religious language. The use of terms such as *love* and *compassion* for God raises the danger of anthropopathism. In what way are God's "feelings" similar to ours? Can one speak analogically of God without being committed to the medieval analogy of being? Of our six theologians, Lee comes the closest

---

[29]Phyllis Trible, *God and the Rhetoric of Sexuality* (Philadelphia: Fortress Press, 1978) 31-59, discusses this term in the context of feminist theology.

[30]John A. T. Robinson, *The New Reformation?* (Philadelphia: Westminster, 1965) 112-14.

to a systematic inquiry into this subject.[31] Perhaps the sorrow and passion of God can become the focus of as much meaningful theological dialogue as past generations devoted to the wrath of God.

Second, a theology of divine suffering must be aware of the interaction between faith, culture, and experience. The theologians assembled here generally agree that traditional Christian theism unfortunately was wedded to a particular philosophical system early in its history. The concern to de-Hellenize Christian theology appears in several of our authors. Perhaps authors from an Eastern background (Lee, Kitamori) or a black heritage (Cone) can see a dimension of the Christian faith often overlooked by theologians trained in the tradition of impassibility. Sometimes these authors tend to set up traditional Western theism as a straw man for their attacks, but they have been able to step outside the mainstream and see a valuable aspect of the Christian faith. One does not have to adopt the metaphysical principles of the *I ching* (Lee) or A. N. Whitehead (Williams) to be able to appreciate that the Bible speaks directly to the issue of divine passion. Also, one does not have to reject all metaphysics in order to recover the biblical emphasis on divine compassion. Probably a variety of metaphysical systems would allow for an emphasis on God's identity with human misery. None of the six we have studied would propose a radical dichotomy between the "God of Abraham, Isaac, and Jacob" and the "God of the philosophers." They simply are questioning the unfortunate linking of concepts of God such as Aristotle's unmoved mover with the Christian conception.

Authors such as Cone, Lee, and Kitamori alert us to the value of personal experience and culture in theological reflection. Members of the dominant class in American culture, for example, have a hard time conceiving of a suffering God; but someone like Cone, from the oppressed minority, much more readily notes the biblical emphasis on God's concern for the oppressed. Only in the last few years have white, male, North Atlantic theologians begun to re-

---

[31]C. S. Lewis has helpfully distinguished several meanings of love in relation to God in *The Problem of Pain* (New York: Macmillan, 1962) 37-54, and *The Four Loves* (New York: Harcourt Brace Jovanovich, 1960).

alize how limited their theological perspectives have been. It is not accidental that three of the theologians studied were from outside traditional academic circles (Lee, Kitamori, Cone). Moltmann, MacGregor, and Williams were exceptional in the way they transcended their identity with the majority culture. Certainly a culture such as ours that tends to value self-assurance and success will not quickly recognize a God who is vulnerable and compassionate. Perhaps one of the factors that has prevented a real appreciation for the suffering-God concept in our country is the tendency to highlight divine power to the neglect of divine love. Although academic theologians have been reluctant until this century to affirm divine suffering, a study of Christian piety, especially through its devotional writings and hymnody, would probably reveal a greater willingness among lay people to accept divine suffering. This apparent divergence between professional opinion and Christian experience might be due to the lay person's lack of familiarity with the philosophical presuppositions that led to the impassibility doctrine.

Third, a theology of divine suffering should fit within the context of a serious rethinking of the God-world relationship. I indicated in the section of this chapter on "Providence and the Passion of God" that these six theologians did not successfully deal with issues such as the origin of evil and the distribution of evil. These issues are only two among many that need the careful attention of theologians sympathetic to divine suffering. The affirmation of divine passion might be the starting point for a systematic reconsideration of the doctrine of God. Moltmann has helpfully located his view of the crucified God within the context of an eschatological theology of history. Lee, in his *God Suffers for Us*, relates the *agape* nature of God to a variety of theological issues. MacGregor also focuses on the relation of divine kenosis to several themes, such as prayer.

I agree that many discussions of theodicy and providence are so speculative and theoretical that they do not provide existential help to the sufferer. I would suggest, however, that theologians need to draw out the implications of divine suffering for other theological issues. Recognizing that "the job of the theologian is not to unscrew the inscrutable,"[32] the theologian still must not be guilty of treating themes and issues in isolation.

Fourth, a theology of divine suffering should have implications for the Christian life and Christian ministry. Going back to the passage in Corinthians cited earlier, we note that Paul tells those Christians that because they have encountered the God of compassion and comfort they are to help others, "so that we can comfort those in any trouble with the comfort we ourselves have received from God" (2 Corinthians 1:4 NIV). Indeed, throughout the Bible there is a clear emphasis on an imitation of God by believers. If God is compassionate, then his followers should be compassionate. God's compassion is frequently cited as a motivation for our human compassion. The passage cited earlier (Exodus 22:27) identifying God as compassionate comes in the context of an admonition to the Hebrews to treat the poor humanely (Exodus 22:21-27). Luke's account of the so-called Sermon on the Plain includes, "Be compassionate as your Father is compassionate" (Luke 6:36 NEB).

As we saw in the section on "The Wounded Healers" in this chapter, several proponents of divine passion see the relevance of this doctrine for the Christian's life in the world. Moltmann and Cone have probably done the most thoughtful work here, encouraging Christians to be sensitive to the needs of suffering humanity. A compassionate, loving God expects his people to be actively involved in ministering to a hurting world. A full discussion of the compassionate, empathetic Christian life-style is beyond the scope of this book, but one example might help.[33] An appreciation of divine suffering might help Christians establish their priorities for individual and corporate ministry. Christians, like the God they follow, should be sensitive to any human suffering, but limited resources need careful allocation. No one can quantify human suf-

---

[32]Robert Farrar Capon, *The Third Peacock: The Goodness of God and the Badness of the World* (Garden City NY: Image, 1972) 59.

[33]For a more devotional approach to this theme, see Donald P. McNeill, Douglas A. Morrison, and Henri J. M. Nouwen, *Compassion: A Reflection on the Christian Life* (Garden City NY: Doubleday, 1982).

fering very precisely, but the distribution of human resources in response to human suffering should be compassionate as well as prudent. Sadly, some Christians have devoted many resources to causes that had little to do with the alleviation of human suffering. A God who grieves over human sin and human pain must also sorrow over the failure of Christians to heed his example.

A PROBLEM THAT WILL NOT REST

The question of the passion of God is "a problem that will not rest in the Christian mind and conscience."[34] Most Christian theologians have followed the traditional impassibility position, perhaps partly due to the fear of the patripassianist heresy or due to a simple failure to examine the issue carefully. Although I have focused primarily on six proponents of divine passion rather than its critics, the debate is certainly not over. As I noted at the end of the first chapter, there are several arguments for divine impassibility. In this final chapter I have suggested that these new "patripassianists" need to clarify and amplify their positions in order to further support their crucial insights.

Does God suffer? The answer of most theologians in Christian history would be an unequivocal "no." The six theologians we have examined, however, would answer with a resounding "yes." This latter reply reflects a deeply rooted concern among contemporary theologians to develop an authentically Christian understanding of God. Indeed, as Dietrich Bonhoeffer suggested: "The Bible directs man to God's powerlessness and suffering; only the suffering God can help."[35] That so many can now argue the passion of God constitutes a remarkable "structural shift in the Christian mind" of the twentieth century.[36] Each of these six theologians understands the passion of God in a different way, but the common denomi-

---

[34]Daniel Day Williams, "The Vulnerable and the Invulnerable God," *Christianity and Crisis* 22 (5 March 1962): 27.

[35]Bonhoeffer, *Letters and Papers from Prison*, 188.

[36]Daniel Day Williams, *What Present Day Theologians Are Thinking*, 3d ed., rev. (New York: Harper & Row, 1967) 172.

nator is that God can and does suffer. Moltmann describes a crucified God who participates in the human struggle for freedom and justice. Cone speaks of the God who identifies with the oppressed of the world. MacGregor's kenotic God suffers along with the world because of his loving self-limitation. Kitamori identifies the pain of God as the struggle he experiences between his love and his wrath. Williams discusses a dipolar God who is both vulnerable to the world's misery and invulnerable to final defeat. Lee develops a view of divine possibility based on God's *agape* nature and his divine empathy.

Does God suffer? The issue can be formulated in a three-word, simple sentence, but it is an issue that will continue to haunt Christians despite these recent discussions. Such a simple question is actually the tip of the proverbial iceberg insofar as its resolution involves a variety of complex theological, biblical, philosophical, and practical issues. To many contemporary Christians, the God who suffers is also the God who heals. Whether such a position is a recovery of a genuinely biblical theme or simply the latest revival of an ancient heresy is open to further debate. A growing number of Christians would opt for the former. Paul Ricoeur once suggested that the "symbol gives rise to the thought."[37] The notion of God as the wounded healer, as the passionate deity, should give rise to further thought. At present the judgment of S. Paul Schilling seems fair: the passion of God is "the most profound of all responses to human anguish."[38]

---

[37]Paul Ricoeur, *The Symbolism of Evil*, trans. Emerson Buchanan (Boston: Beacon Press, 1967) 348.

[38]Schilling, *God and Human Anguish*, 235.

Index